Pandora's Last Voyage

The Board of Admiralty found the *Bounty* mutiny irritating and inopportune. In 1791 the frigate *Pandora* was sent to the Pacific to find the errant ship and bring the mutineers back to justice. The area of search was vast and largely uncharted, and *Pandora* failed to apprehend Fletcher Christian and the main party on the island of Pitcairn. But she managed to round up those of the mutineers who, being sailors, had elected to stay on Tahiti with its obvious charms. There was, however, one embarrassing hindrance to free enjoyment of the island women: the common iron nail was the fee required, and the consequent depredations upon a ship's fabric seriously impaired its seaworthiness.

The prisoners had to face the brutal discipline of *Pandora*'s captain. Innocent and guilty alike were clapped into 'Pandora's Box', an open cage on deck, and some were inexcusably lost, drowned in their manacles, when *Pandora* struck a reef. There ensued an astonishing passage to safety—in open boats, amid tortures of sun, hunger and thirst—but to some safety meant trial, conviction and probable death.

Contemporary documents form the basis of Geoffrey Rawson's lively and laconic account of that voyage, of *Pandora*'s crew and her prisoners, victims of the eighteenth century's penal cruelty: George Stewart who married a Tahitian chief's daughter and whose romance was celebrated by Byron; Mary Bryant, the convict mother from Botany Bay; James Morrison, *Bounty*'s bo'sun, diarist and radical, with the Garter Star tattooed on his chest. Here too are the friendly people of the 'Island Paradises' to whom the coming of ships' crews brought little but sorrow and degradation. Set against a background of perilous reefs and blue uncharted seas, this exciting episode in our naval history has all the pace and suspense of an adventure story.

THE AUTHOR

Geoffrey Rawson, who was educated at Christ's Hospital, began his seafaring life with more than three years in sail before joining the Royal Indian Marine. He first went to Australia during the 1914–18 War, and after returning to England for a tour of duty as Naval Liaison Officer he went back to Australia to make his home near Melbourne.

His previous books include *Bligh of the* Bounty, *Mary Bryant* and *Desert Journey*.

By the same author

BLIGH OF THE *BOUNTY*

MARY BRYANT

DESERT JOURNEYS

SEA PRELUDE

LETTERS FROM LORD NELSON

Pandora's
Last Voyage

Geoffrey Rawson

Longmans

LONGMANS, GREEN AND CO LTD
48 Grosvenor Street, London W.1

*Associated companies, branches and representatives
throughout the world*

© *Geoffrey Rawson 1963*
First published 1963

*Printed in Great Britain by
Jarrold and Sons Ltd, Norwich*

Contents

Illustrations

Maps

Acknowledgements

The principal authorities for the following narrative are the contemporary accounts by:

Captain E. Edwards, commanding HMS *Pandora*: *Reports to the Admiralty*.
Surgeon G. Hamilton: *A Voyage Round the World in HM Frigate* Pandora.
James Morrison, bo'sun's mate: *Morrison's Journal*.
Lieut. G. Mortimer: *Voyage to Tahiti in the brig* Mercury.
James Martin: *Memorandoms*.

I have been unable to trace the copyright owners in *Voyage of HMS* Pandora by E. Edwards, published by F. Edwards and should welcome any information which would enable me to do so.

The Trustees of the Mitchell Library, Sydney, have permitted me to include extracts from the *Journal* of James Morrison, the original of which is in the Mitchell Library.

The Council of the Hakluyt Society have allowed me to include extracts from their publications *The Quest and Occupation of Tahiti* by Bolton Glanvill Corney (1915), and *The Discovery of Tahiti* edited by Hugh Carrington (1948).

Mr Charles Blount has allowed me to use the *Memorandoms* of James Martin which he discovered, edited and printed.

I am indebted to the late Owen Rutter, the author of many books on the subject, and to Dr George Mackaness who devoted many years to his monumental *Life of Vice-Admiral William Bligh*, which is based on original research over a very wide field.

G. R.

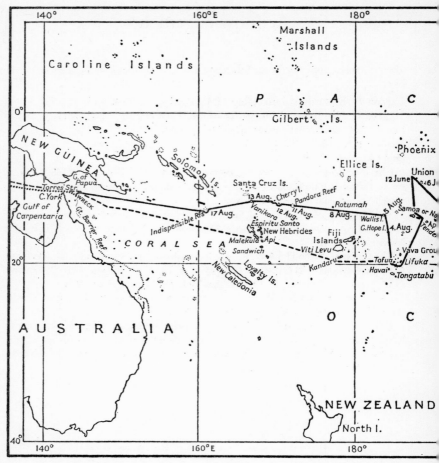

The Pacific Ocean showing the course followed by HMS *Pandora* in 1791. The intersecting tracks between Tonga and Samoa have been omitted.

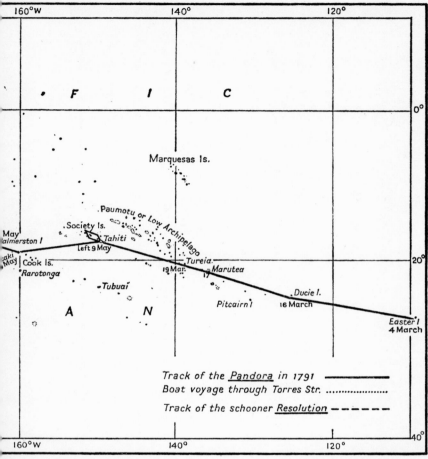

Track of the _Pandora_ in 1791 ─────
Boat voyage through Torres Str. ....
Track of the schooner _Resolution_ ── ── ──

Based upon British Admiralty Chart No. 2693 with the permission of HM Stationery Office and the Hydrographer of the Navy

Part I

Chapter 1

The Voyage Begins

WHEN on 16 March 1790, Lieutenant Bligh arrived at the Admiralty to report the loss of his ship HMS *Bounty* by mutiny, the Board of Admiralty were impressed by his tale.

They complimented him on his courage and resource, agreed to his request to be brought to a court martial so that his honour and ability might be vindicated, and promised him another ship so that he might fulfil his bread-fruit mission so unhappily interrupted.

His strange story, when the details became known, created a sensation and the news of the mutiny flew round the world on the wings of white-sailed ships.

The episode was, however, an irritating incident for the government and for the Admiralty. It came at a most inopportune time. England seemed to be very close to war with Spain, and with France as the ally of Spain. A bitter dispute had arisen over rival claims to Nootka Sound on the north-west coast of America. Spain was provocative; Britain was firm. All naval activities were concentrated on the assembly and equipment of a great fleet under the command of Lord Howe. It included thirty ships of the line, nine frigates and numerous other vessels. Many officers languishing on half-pay set off for London to beg for employment at sea, among them Captain Horatio Nelson.

While Britain thus faced the prospect of a coalition of her enemies, she was at the same time acquiring many possessions overseas and building up her Empire.

The loss of the *Bounty* and the necessity for sending out another ship to recapture her placed a further strain on the existing naval resources. The *Bounty* was but a converted trader with no guns except for a chest of arms. Nevertheless, the *Bounty* mutineers might show fight and it was considered necessary to send out a well-armed vessel, and a fast one.

Furthermore, a successful mutiny would have a bad effect on morale and on the national prestige. There was a possibility that the mutineers might run wild on the high seas, indulge in acts of piracy and involve the

Government in international incidents. They were in fact officially dubbed 'pirates'.

Finally, the area of search was a vast ocean, only very partially explored but known to be studded with thousands of islands and archipelagoes and other suitable hiding-places. As the mutineers were reported to have cried 'Huzza for Otaheite!' it was considered to be highly probable that the *Bounty* and possibly the mutineers as well would be found there, and it was accordingly decided that the search ship should, in the first place, proceed to Tahiti direct.

For the purpose, the Admiralty reluctantly withdrew from the war fleet a valuable frigate mounting twenty-four guns. She was a three-masted ship-rigged vessel, carrying a complement of 160, and named *Pandora*.

The manning, equipment and provisioning of the *Pandora* became a nuisance to those responsible for fitting out the fleet. Naval recruiting at the time was strained to the utmost; stores and equipment were not readily forthcoming, and when received were not of the best quality. Lord Howe's great fleet was absorbing everybody and everything, and the *Pandora*'s crew were chiefly landsmen who had been rounded up by press gangs.

On 10 August, five months after Captain Bligh had reported himself to the Admiralty, Captain Edward Edwards was appointed to the command of the ship. He was an experienced officer, a strict disciplinarian and was evidently regarded at the Admiralty as highly suitable for this particular task. He was then forty-nine years of age, had been a post captain for nine years, had been in action several times, and had been in the Service for more than thirty years.

Like all such single-ship ventures in the eighteenth century, Captain Edwards was faced with a formidable, not to say a hazardous voyage in uncharted waters. He was bound round Cape Horn, into the Pacific with an overcrowded ship and a raw crew on a voyage that might last two years or more, to search for mutineers in a ship that might or might not be afloat. There was little chance of honour and glory on such a mission, whereas in Lord Howe's fleet he might have distinguished himself in action and had a chance of prize money.

Captain Edwards' sailing orders[1] were clear and explicit.

He was directed to round Cape Horn and to steer directly for Matavai Bay, Tahiti, where it was thought the mutineers might most probably be found. If he did not find them there, he was to visit the Society and

[1] Vide Edwards' sailing orders. Adm. 2/120. P.R.O.

Friendly Islands, and other known islands in the neighbourhood. If he apprehended the pirates, he was to 'keep them as closely confined as may preclude all possibility of their escaping, having proper regard to the preservation of their lives that they may be brought home to undergo the punishment due to their demerits'.

On his return passage, Edwards was directed to examine and survey Endeavour Strait, between Australia and New Guinea, returning to England round the Cape.

He seems to have been conscious of the fact that the task of searching the ocean would be beyond him. In his report to the Admiralty, he subsequently wrote:

Christian had been frequently heard to declare that he would search for an unknown or uninhabited island in which there was no harbour for shipping, would run the ship ashore, and get from her such things as would be useful to him and settle there, but this information was too vague to be followed by me in an immense ocean strewed with an almost innumerable number of known and unknown islands.

Nevertheless, it had been fully impressed upon him by the Admiralty that this was not to be an exploring expedition through an immense ocean strewn with innumerable islands, but a police mission to capture and to bring back alive the wicked desperado Fletcher Christian and his pirate gang. Christian was the supreme villain, Captain Bligh the national hero.

But in some strange way, a gradual metamorphosis later took place in the popular imagination. The villain became the hero, the hero the villain. As time passed, the figure of Captain Bligh became invested in a sinister light as a cruel, heartless bully while that of Fletcher Christian was endowed with all the charm of a romantic adventurer, a role which was heightened by the poets of the time. Christian, it appeared, was the type of man of whom women's heroes are made. Even that 'young and timid female' as she described herself, Mary Russell Mitford confessed that she was 'irresistibly attracted by the character of the young and amiable Christian', and lauded him in her poem, 'Christina'. She portrayed him falling to the seductive charms of the sister of the local tribal chief:

> His passion soared on eagle wing
> He loved the sister of the King.

wrote the infatuated poetess.

In his poem 'The Island', Byron glamorized the story of the *Bounty*.

For this was a genuine, a highly dramatic mutiny. It was a swift *coup d'état*, no sooner conceived than executed; within half an hour the whole thing was over.

Now, Captain Edwards was faced with the task of finding and bringing home the mutineers to undergo the customary and inevitable punishment. This was a frightful fate, worse, if possible, than to be hanged, drawn and quartered. There was no quick drop, no sudden extinction, but the slow agony of strangulation as the victim was run up to the yard-arm by his shipmates, on the order being given, twisting and turning as he was slowly choked to death.

*   *   *

Although Captain Edwards had a scratch crew enlisted or pressed from many sources, he seems to have been provided with first-rate officers and warrant officers. The first lieutenant, John Larkan, was a seasoned officer who in a short time produced a smart disciplined ship's company in difficult and uncomfortable conditions. He has been accused of being harsh if not downright cruel, like his captain, but those were harsh times at sea.

The second lieutenant, Robert Corner, was undoubtedly a most efficient and humane officer. Captain Edwards appointed him Landing Officer, in which capacity he made all the boat landings at the Pacific Islands. The *Pandora*'s doctor praises him several times while ignoring Larkan altogether, and he seems to have been a more tender-hearted man in contrast to his two seniors.

In addition, there were on board two lieutenants recently promoted from midshipman, Thomas Hayward and John Hallett. They had been midshipmen in the *Bounty* and had been commended by Bligh. They knew all the mutineers, all about the mutiny, all about the islanders. In addition, Hayward was a navigator and familiar with Tahitian waters. The sailing master of the *Pandora* was George Passmore, also a competent surveyor and navigator and, unlike the *Bounty*, the *Pandora* carried a purser, Gregory Bentham, who had sailed with Captain Cook and was familiar with Tahiti.

It is significant also that the *Pandora* carried a detachment of Marines, Captain Bligh having stated that if he had had some Marines on board the *Bounty*, Fletcher Christian would not have been so easily successful.

The *Pandora* carried a surgeon, George Hamilton, who is principally interesting as the author of a small volume in which he described the voyage of the *Pandora* and what happened in the course of it. His title is not quite accurate as the *Pandora* did not complete a voyage round the world, though her company did.[1]

*   *   *

At length all was ready, and on 7 November 1790, eight months since Captain Bligh had reported himself, the *Pandora* sailed from Portsmouth on her mission.

Surgeon Hamilton described the departure:

Everything necessary being completed, we dropped down to Sheerness and, after passing the Downs, arrived at Portsmouth where we found Lord Howe with the Union Flag at the main, and the proudest navy that ever graced the British seas under his command.

Here the officers and men received six months pay in advance, and after receiving their final orders, got the timekeeper[2] on board, weighed anchor and proceeded to sea.

As the white cliffs of Albion receded from our view, alternate hopes and fears took possession of our minds, wafting the last kind adieu to our native soil.

[1] Hamilton. *A Voyage Round the World in His Majesty's frigate* Pandora.
[2] The chronometer for navigating and determining longitude.

Chapter 2

Spain Claims the Pacific

W HEN Captain Edwards set forth for Tahiti, nearly a quarter of a century had passed since its discovery in 1767 by Captain Wallis[1] in the *Dolphin*. Twenty European ships had visited it in the interval, and it was now well known.

Wallis had named it King George III Island, and had taken possession in the name of that monarch. Then came the French ships *Boudeuse* and *Etoile* under Bougainville who took possession in the name of the French king. Then came Cook in the *Endeavour Bark* for the purpose of observing the Transit of Venus.

These penetrations of seas and lands over which the King of Spain claimed exclusive sovereignty alarmed the Spanish authorities. Within a month of the arrival of the *Dolphin* in the Thames, the Spanish Ambassador at the Court of St James's was writing to the Minister of State in Madrid.

Most Excellent Señor,

As a result of the measures taken by the French embassy and myself to ascertain clearly where the islands publicly stated here to have been discovered by Capt. Wallace are situated, we have managed to come across a seaman out of his own ship, the *Dolphin*, who has promised to supply us with a very circumstantial journal of his voyage. The person through whom we got him to speak has had several conversations with him, and according to the information he has given him – for the truth and accuracy of which he says he will vouch his head – it seems that we cannot doubt but that the islands the aforesaid Wallace claims to have

[1] Some geographers and most encyclopedias regard Tahiti as having been first discovered by Fernandez de Quiros in 1606. The island discovered by de Quiros is now generally believed to be Anaa or Chain Island, so named by Cook, in the same latitude as Tahiti but 200 miles east of it. The topographical discrepancies are too great to identify one with the other, and de Quiros' facilities for finding his longitude too meagre and inaccurate. More than a century and a half after de Quiros, Boenechea and Captain Cook both charted Anaa or Chain Island. Cook's longitude was twenty-five miles too far west, and Boenechea's no less than 5° 41′ too far east. In any case, Anaa or Chain Island could not be Tahiti since the former is an atoll with lagoon and the latter lofty, mountainous and volcanic.

discovered are the same that were seen in the year 1605 by Quiros under whose name they appear in the English atlases.

This seaman, who has served in Spain in the ship *Glorioso* being now discontented with the service under his own nation, wishes to return to ours; it was with that object in view and by the aid of a small gratuity given him that he has supplied the information for which he was asked.

I do not know in what capacity he aspires to enter our service; if as a mere seaman, there need be no difficulty in admitting him, but there might be some in making him a Master. He has only explained that he has a lively wish to serve in Spain without particularising anything else.

Meanwhile it will be necessary to contribute towards his support and this I am intending to do.

They have just brought me this man's Journal, a copy of which I herewith transmit. After having read it attentively, it appears to me that the islands Capt. Wallace has been at can be no other than those discovered by Quiros.

May God preserve Your Excy many years, as is my desire.

London 24 June 1768.

Most Exct Señor &c &c.

To

El Principe de Masserano

The Most Exct Sr Marqs de Grimaldi.[1]

In consequence of this information, the Spanish authorities subsequently dispatched the frigate *Aguila* to Tahiti under the command of Captain Domingo de Boenechea to investigate.

But already the *Dolphin*'s visit had been followed by the arrival of the two French ships, and by Captain Cook's expedition to Tahiti in 1769. Thus, when Boenechea arrived at Tahiti in 1772, more than five and a half years had elapsed since Wallis had first discovered the island, and in the interval French and British ships had been there and raised their respective flags. Since Spain claimed sovereignty over the whole Pacific region and since the British and French expeditions were well known to the Spanish authorities, they do not appear to have taken early and effective steps to uphold their claims.

The visit of Boenechea in 1772 lasted only one month, and was followed by that of Cook on his Second Voyage in *Resolution*, *Adventure* commanded by Captain Furneaux in 1773 and a visit by Cook in the *Resolution* in 1774. A few months later Boenechea arrived again in the *Aguila*. She remained six weeks (1774–5) during which time Boenechea died and was buried there.

Two years later, in 1777, Cook arrived at Tahiti on his third and last voyage with *Resolution* and *Discovery*.

[1] Corney, Quest and Occupation of Tahiti.

He inspected some Spanish buildings and other signs of Spanish occupation, including the grave of Boenechea, which lay at the foot of a large cross which had been erected in token of Spanish possession. This large cross bore a conspicuous carved inscription

CAROLUS III IMPERAT 1774

To make it quite clear to all and sundry that Tahiti was not the possession of Charles III of Spain but of George III of Great Britain, Captain Cook had the cross taken down and on the opposite side to the Spanish inscription was carved in equally large letters

GEORGIUS TERTIUS. REX. ANNIS
1767. 1769. 1773. 1774. 1777.

these being the dates of the visits by British ships.

The cross was then re-erected.

All trace of the cross and the grave had vanished a few years later.

The main purpose of the Spanish Government at this period was to maintain her absolute claims to all the Pacific Ocean and all the territories therein, and to exclude every foreign power and every foreigner from trading or establishing a foothold there, and in general to exercise a complete monopoly there.

The main purpose of the English, and of other governments, was to challenge and to defeat all such claims and for this purpose a succession of expeditions was sent into the Pacific. The basic reason for all such enterprises was clearly indicated by the official instructions issued to Captain John Byron RN of the *Dolphin* in 1765 :

Whereas nothing can redound more to the honour of this Nation as a Maritime Power, to the Dignity of the Crown and to the advancement of Trade and Navigation thereof than to make Discoveries of Countries hitherto unknown, and to attain a perfect knowledge of the distant Parts of the British Empire which though formerly discovered by His Majesty's subjects have been as yet but imperfectly explored. . . .

Here we see the process of the building up of the British Empire in operation and the term *Empire* in use, a process initiated by Drake and continued by his successors, Cavendish, Narborough, Hawkins, Grenville, Raleigh and company. The result was that the so-called exclusive domain of Spain was so penetrated and infested by British ships that in the end Spain no longer had any foothold at all in the Pacific and, with some exceptions, the whole ocean came under British control.

The Pacific Ocean became a British ocean, spotted with innumerable islands and island groups marked in red.

And not only the ocean.

The great South American continent lay open to British capital and the capitalists, avid to break the Spanish monopoly, thrust their way into the rich investment territories of the continent and set up the great commercial and mining enterprises.

But only for a century – the nineteenth and early part of the twentieth – until two great wars. Britain had ousted Spain. Now the United States ousted Britain.

'Westward the course of Empire takes its way', and this phrase chimed with the tradition inherited from Hawkins, Drake, Raleigh and Cromwell.

*　　*　　*

The *Bounty* expedition and the *Pandora* mission were exceptions to this colonizing and acquisitive campaign of the English. Neither was sent out with any exploring and colonizing mission, except to acquire such unconsidered trifles as might be snapped up *en route*, as Edwards did.

The *Bounty* was dispatched with a specific purpose and with one object only – to transplant bread-fruit from Tahiti to the West Indies.

The *Pandora*'s mission was even more limited, to apprehend and to bring back the mutineers.

Sir Basil Thomson in his Introduction to the *Voyage of HMS Pandora* took a dim view of Captain Edwards' conduct of the expedition. Both Bligh and Edwards have been subjected to severe criticism, but the character and conduct of these two insignificant figures in our long island story are of little consequence. Compared with the Drakes and the Hawkinses, the Raleighs and Cooks, they were pygmies. They owed their fame or notoriety simply to the fact that they were the principal actors in a minor episode in our naval annals which, however, was sufficiently sensational to excite the imagination and to capture the public interest.

Sir Basil Thomson, writing in 1915, complains that Captain Edwards was 'almost the worst man that could have been chosen, having no imagination or interest beyond the straitened limits of his profession'. But the naval profession, in those times at least, had no straitened limits. The whole world was open to the naval profession and once a ship was hull down, she passed any straitened limits into the blue, free from Admiralty control or support.

Sir Basil Thomson opined that 'a more genial man would have written a Journal of discovery that might have taken a place in the front rank of the literature of travel'. The Admiralty in the eighteenth century was hardly a travel bureau. If geniality and the writing of travel literature are among the primary aims and principal duties of Captains RN, the criticism might be justified, but the general view, now as then, is that the principal function of a Captain RN is not to write travel literature but to command his ship and to carry out his orders.

'From the point of view of the Admiralty,' wrote Sir Basil, 'the cruise was intended simply as a police mission without any scientific object', and he then castigates Captain Edwards for not attempting to occupy 'the front rank of the literature of travel'. Captain Edwards did not share this prolific writer's itch for the literature of travel and left the task to his surgeon to give the world an account of the *Pandora*'s voyage.

Nor is it quite clear what Sir Basil's qualifications were for instructing a captain in his duties, in the eighteenth century. He himself as a young man had served in the colonial service in Fiji and Tonga, but most of his career was spent in the prison service and in Scotland Yard, 'that useful class of public service that lives upon instructions' as he himself defines it.

Sir Basil Thomson states that 'Edwards had a roving commission in an ocean studded with undiscovered islands'. If there was one instruction omitted from Edwards' sailing orders, it was to go a-roving, yet Thomson says the Admiralty intended the cruise simply as a police mission and then terms it a roving commission.

Chapter 3

Pandora Arrives

No sooner had the *Pandora* cleared the Channel than a 'malignant fever' made itself felt and thirty-five men were soon on the sick list. The ship was overcrowded, even the cabins being filled with provisions and stores. Fifteen days after leaving England, she anchored in Santa Cruz, Tenerife where Edwards refilled his water butts, took on board three months' wine for the ship's company, together with fruit and vegetables. He sailed again on 25 November and arrived at Rio de Janeiro on 31 December 1790.

I anchored here with a view to compleat my water and get refreshments for the ship's company. I am persuaded that very long runs particularly with new ships' companies are prejudicial to health and as my men have suffered in their health from a fever which has prevailed among them in a greater or less degree ever since they left England were other inducements for my touching at this port.

The surgeon, George Hamilton, mentions

the uncommon good effects we experienced from supplying the sick and con-valescent with tea and sugar, this being the first time it has ever been introduced into his Majesty's service. . . . It will be sought with more avidity by those whose aliment consists chiefly in animal food, and that always salt and often of the worst kind. Our bread, too, is generally mixed with oatmeal and of a hot drying nature. Scarcity of water is a calamity to which seafaring people are always subject and it is an established fact that a pint of tea will satiate thirst more than a quart of water. . . . Quartermasters and real good seamen going long voyages always make it an article in their agreement to be supplied with tea and sugar.

On 8 January 1791, the *Pandora* left Rio bound round the Horn. Before rounding the Horn, Captain Edwards would have liked to have put in at one last harbour for refreshing his men before beginning the long run to Tahiti:

but as I arrived too late on that coast to fulfil my intentions within the time, it determined me to push forward without delay, by which means I flattered myself I might avoid that extreme bad weather and all the evil consequences usually experienced in doubling Cape Horn in a more advanced season of the year.

Surgeon Hamilton notes that, after rounding the Horn and entering the Pacific

the weather became exceedingly pleasant and the many good things with which we were supplied began to have a wonderful effect on our convalescents. The sour crout was often eaten as a salad with vinegar in preference to cut vegetables from the shore. A cask of this grand antiscorbutic was kept open for the crew to eat as much as they pleased. The Essence of Malt afforded a delightful beverage and with the addition of a little hops in the warmest climates made as good strong beer as we could in England.[1] Cocoa we found great benefit from; it is the only article of nourishment in sea victualling, for what can in reason be expected from beef or pork after it has been salted a year or two. The men were extremely fond of meat, rough ground in a mill, with a little brown sugar; we availed ourselves at every opportunity of baking soft bread for half the complement at a time. . . .

The dividing the people into three watches had a double good effect as it gave them longer time to sleep, and dry themselves before they turned in, and as most of our crew consisted of landsmen, the fewer there were on watch at a time rendered it necessary to exert themselves more in learning their duty.

When the *Pandora* entered the Pacific bound for Tahiti, she was following in the wake of a number of predecessors. Among them were:

HMS *Dolphin* (Capt. Wallis RN)	1767
French frigate *Boudeuse* (Bougainville)	1768
HMS *Endeavour Bark* (Capt. Cook)	1769
Spanish frigate *Aguila* (Boenechea)	1772
HMS *Resolution* (Capt. Cook)	1773
HMS *Adventure* (Capt. Furneaux)	1773
HMS *Resolution* (Capt. Cook)	1774
Spanish frigate *Aguila* (Boenechea)	1774–5
HMS *Resolution* (Capt. Cook)	1777
HMS *Discovery* (Capt. Clerke)	1777

There followed an interval of eleven years without any European visit to Tahiti. Then came:

[1] The beer was usually so superior to the water in those days that 'water allowance' was paid to the crew to compensate the men for having to drink water because of shortage of beer.

Transport *Lady Penrhyn*	1788
HMS *Bounty* (Capt. Bligh)	1788
Brig *Mercury* (Capt. Cox)	1789
HMS *Pandora* (Capt. Edwards)	1791

The track from the Horn or Magellan Straits to Tahiti was a well-known, if not yet a well-beaten, track. Most of the expeditions had entered the Pacific Ocean from the west, following in the wake of Magellan, and most of them had found that the prevailing winds were westerly and strong. Even if the difficult Magellan Strait was successfully negotiated, or the open sea route round the Horn was accomplished, in those high latitudes in 50° south, the winds were still westerly and strong, forcing ships to the north as soon as they entered the Pacific. The consequence was that the immense stretch of open ocean lying between 30° and 50° south was not penetrated, being practically inaccessible for sailing ships. The immense region between South America and New Zealand remained unknown and unexplored and was generally believed to contain a Great South Land, until Captain Cook finally cruised in that region and found no land at all.

In any case, Captain Edwards had no mandate for exploring the ocean. His immediate goal was Tahiti and the way there led past Easter Island, and Ducie's Island, the latter now first discovered and named.

Sir Basil Thomson seems to imply that by not altering course due west from Ducie's Island, Edwards made a grave mistake:[1] 'Had he sailed due west from Ducie Island, he *must* have sighted Pitcairn Island and discovered the hiding-place of Fletcher Christian's ill-fated colony.'

Owen Rutter repeats the idea. 'Had he but sailed due West after passing Ducie Island, he would have sighted Pitcairn Island and might have taken Christian and his companions before ever reaching Tahiti.'

This is a large assumption. Why should Edwards have altered course at this time? The course to Tahiti was west-north-west, not due west, and Edwards' orders were to proceed direct to Tahiti. Captain Edwards did not know, as Thomson and Rutter both knew, that the mutineers were on Pitcairn. Furthermore, Edwards might have passed Pitcairn in the dark hours, or during a rain squall, fog or mist. Landing on Pitcairn is almost impossible except in fine weather. There is no safe or convenient anchorage, and no doubt Christian and his men would have at once concealed

[1] Sir Basil Thomson states: 'The first land sighted after rounding Cape Horn was Ducie's Island,' but Surgeon Hamilton says: 'On 4th March we saw Easter Island,' Ducie's Island not being seen until 16 March.

themselves on sighting a British frigate approaching. Nor would Pitcairn have been easily found, for though it is a bold landmark by day, rising to 1,000 feet, the discoverer of the island, Captain Carteret, had placed it on the chart nearly 200 miles too far west.

Had Edwards headed for Pitcairn and located the pirates there, the task of apprehending them, alive, had they shown fight, might have been a ticklish one. The *Pandora* mounted a devastating broadside of guns, but of what benefit would a bombardment of the island be? He could have landed strong armed parties, but landing itself, except in calm weather, is hazardous and it might have been fiercely opposed by nine armed and desperate men. The concentration of their fire on the *Pandora*'s boats as they approached the difficult landing-place would have been very effective.

Captain Edwards would have been a helpless spectator, concerned with the safety of his ship and obliged to keep a good offing. The official anchorage, shown on the chart, is in eighteen fathoms with rocky bottom, on the weather side of the island and fewer than four cables from a lee shore.

Captain Sir Thomas Staines RN reported:

The coast affords no shelter for a ship or vessel of any description. The island is completely iron-bound with rocky shores and the landing in boats must be at all times difficult, although the island may be safely approached within a short distance by a ship.

Not a very comfortable base from which to conduct such an operation as the capture of the mutineers, alive. Sir Basil Thomson adds: 'Relentless ill-fortune turned the *Pandora* northward.' But neither relentless ill-fortune, nor anything else 'turned' the *Pandora* northward. She did not, in point of fact, 'turn' at all. The ship was running free on a west-north-west course with the south-east trade wind astern, on a direct course for Tahiti, and had no occasion to 'turn' from that course. Everything seemed to be going well. She was now approaching her destination in fine weather with blue skies and calm seas. The air, says the surgeon, was temperate, mild and agreeable.

Captain Edwards had already discovered, named and placed on the chart three unknown islands; and all hands were in good health, after being cooped up in the ship for more than four months.

The fever which had prevailed on board gradually declined and the diseases usually succeeding such fevers prevented by a liberal use of the antiscorbutics and other nourishing and useful articles with which we were so amply supplied.

The ship's company arrived at Otaheite in perfect health except a few whose debilitated constitutions no climate, provisions or medicine could much improve.

On 22 March, 136 days after her departure from England, Tahiti was sighted. On the morning of 23 March, in the early dawn light, the *Pandora* under shortened sail crept into Matavai Bay and anchored.

Even before he dropped anchor, Captain Edwards was boarded by several people from the shore who brought him tidings, part welcome and part disturbing. The *Bounty* was not there.

Chapter 4

Fletcher Christian

IF the *Bounty* was not at Tahiti where was she? When Christian ejected Bligh and his party and set them adrift in the boat, he had no idea of his next step. Everything had come about too suddenly for any prearranged plan. Now he was confronted with the immediate problem of what to do, where to go.

The general impression seems to have been that most of the pirates would like to return to Tahiti where they had spent so many pleasant months. But Christian, the leader, had other thoughts. There were two serious objections to a return to Tahiti. One was that, sooner or later, a search vessel would be dispatched to look for them, and the obvious place to begin the search was Tahiti. They would all be captured.

Secondly, in these latitudes, the prevailing wind is easterly and he would have a long beat back to Tahiti. Finally, his early return to Tahiti, and without Captain Bligh and his party – or the bread-fruit plants – would cause the islanders to ask all kinds of awkward questions.

His first business was to organize a new ship's routine. George Stewart, midshipman, was promoted and placed in charge of one watch, while Christian took the other, and James Morrison, bo'sun's mate, was made bo'sun. No one disputed Christian's assumption of the command and he took complete control. The 800 tubs, pots and boxes with the bread-fruit and other plants were dumped over the side. Christian installed himself in Bligh's cabin, to which the arms chest was removed and Christian's 'trusty' A.B. Churchill made his bed upon it.

Christian did not wholly trust all his men and he realized that the instant success of the mutiny was largely, if not wholly, due to the prior possession of the arms chest.

After studying the chart, he at length decided to make for Tubuai Island, nearly 400 miles south of Tahiti, where he hoped to make a permanent settlement. The mutiny had taken place on 28 April and it was not until 28 May that the *Bounty* arrived there. But somehow, Tubuai did not turn out to be such a pleasant spot as they had expected. The natives were not friendly and, unlike the Tahitians, did not like sharing their wives with the newcomers. Discontent increased, the crew demanding more grog and more women, and there were some serious affrays with the islanders who were entirely hostile. In view of this warlike reception, Christian put to sea again and made sail for Tahiti, where he arrived on 6 June, much to the surprise of the islanders. The *Bounty* had sailed on 4 April, homeward bound with the bread-fruit. Now, only two months later, she was back again, but with neither Bligh nor the bread-fruit.

Christian had warned his men not to mention Tubuai to any of the Tahitians, threatened to shoot any deserter on recapture, and he distributed the 'trade' among the crew to make the best market they could. As for shooting would-be deserters among his men, he could well afford to be rid of one or two, and particularly those who secretly desired to dissociate themselves from the mutiny, but he could not afford to run the risk that any such men might later give information concerning his whereabouts when the search ship arrived. For it is a sign of his will-power, determination and dogged ruthlessness that he had not changed his original plan to settle permanently at Tubuai and to crush the islanders' hostility.

As for the friendly Tahitians and their bombardment of questions, Christian pitched a curious yarn to them.

We met Captain Cook and he had taken Mr. Bligh and the others with the plants and the long boat, and he has sent us back to get hogs, goats, etc., for a new settlement which King George had sent him to make, which he described to be on New Holland.

None of the *Bounty*'s men dared to contradict this yarn, knowing that if they said anything contrary, it would soon reach Christian's ears, for the Tahitians were not remarkable for keeping secrets.

Christian, in reply to further questions, said that Captain Cook was waiting for them at Aitutaki. Strangely enough, his fabricated story easily passed with the innocent Tahitians, who did not know that Captain Cook was dead. And as Christian told them that Captain Cook would return to Tahiti as soon as he had completed his business at Aitutaki, they were well content.

Christian was beloved by the Tahitians and Captain Cook was revered by them. All their requests for food and livestock were speedily granted and, after a stay of fourteen days, Christian sailed again with 460 hogs, fifty goats and some native men and women.

The *Bounty* arrived back at Tubuai on 26 June 1789, and Christian was agreeably surprised to find the natives much more friendly. Preparations were at once begun to establish a permanent settlement, the *Bounty* was warped close inshore, the stock landed, sails unbent, yards sent down and a site for a fort chosen.

But now fresh quarrels broke out with the natives, discontent increased, the crew demanding more grog and more women until, at length, on 10 September Christian called all hands to a conference. One of the crew moved that they should return to Tahiti, 'so that they might get women without force'. Sixteen voted in favour, and eight against.

The important agreement was then reached that the sixteen who had voted to stay in Tahiti should be provided with arms and ammunition and an equal share per man of everything in the ship. The *Bounty* was to be left to Christian and his following of eight men. This arrangement discloses the sharp difference of opinion that existed on board. Some of the sixteen, notably the two midshipmen, Heywood and Stewart, the bo'sun Morrison, and Norman, Coleman, McIntosh and Byrne, the blind fiddler, seemed to have had a strong sense of their innocence of the mutiny, but Christian and his party realized they were fugitives from justice.

One week after this all-important conference had settled, once and for all, the unsettled plans of the mutineers, the *Bounty* was ready to leave Tubuai for good. But as the preparations for departure proceeded, the inhabitants of Tubuai became more and more warlike. Open warfare broke out and developed into a battle when an armed party of the mutineers went out to collect the livestock and bring it on board. The bo'sun, Morrison, says there were 700 natives armed with clubs, spears and stones. Several affrays followed and the Tubuaians were finally subdued only after many had been killed and wounded and the *Bounty*'s muskets had done their work. Twenty armed and determined men, it seemed, were ample to defeat hundreds of natives on their home ground. When the *Bounty* at length sailed, she had on board a young Tubuaian chief, Taroa, three others, and twelve Tubuaian women. They had collaborated with the *Bounty*'s men and had to leave the island with them, or remain behind and be killed by their outraged countrymen.

On 20 September 1789, the *Bounty* once again anchored in Matavai Bay. Here the crew split into two parties, sixteen settling down on shore, the remainder staying in the ship with Christian.[1]

---

[1] According to Sir Basil Thomson, they 'fell out among themselves, half taking the *Bounty* to Pitcairn and half remaining at Tahiti'. But nine is not half of twenty-five, nor did they 'fall out'. On the contrary. Matters were settled quite amicably and a fair division of the arms and stores was made, per head. Far from falling out, Christian landed and said farewell to the shore party. For the last time, he accepted full responsibility for the mutiny, and exonerated everybody, including his own adherents, from even suggesting the fatal act.

On board the *Bounty* as she prepared to sail for 'destination unknown', were the nine white men, the young Tubuaian chief, Taroa, and his three friends, 'now very fond of Mr. Christian'.

James Morrison, the bo'sun, gives the total number on board the *Bounty* when she sailed away, including some Tahitian people, as thirty-five. The whites were careful to embark at least a dozen women so that there would be no shortage.

On the following morning, 21 September 1789, the *Bounty* was seen standing out from Matavai Bay, and was soon hull down.

Chapter 5

Pitcairn Island

THE most important news that greeted Captain Edwards when he arrived in Matavai Bay in the *Pandora* was that the *Bounty* was not at Tahiti and that nine of the mutineers had sailed away in her. We now know that Christian had decided to make for Pitcairn Island, but how did he know of the existence of this island and how could he have shaped a course for Pitcairn when he did not know where it was?

In Captain Bligh's bookcase in the *Bounty*, there was included *An Account of the Voyages for making Discoveries in the Southern Hemisphere* by John Hawkesworth, 1773, including an account of the voyage made by Captain Philip Carteret, RN, in the sloop *Swallow*, twenty years earlier. After the mutiny, Christian had studied this book and the chart, and seems to have concluded that this was the very hide-away he was looking for. It was well off the beaten track, far away, remote, isolated. Captain Carteret had not landed on it, but reported that it was well wooded. Unknown to Christian, there was one serious drawback. According to Captain Carteret, the island lay in latitude 25° 2′ S. and longitude 133° 21′ W. of Greenwich. This latitude was reasonably accurate, being ascertained by a simple calculation based on the sun's altitude at noon, but to ascertain the longitude of such a speck in a distant ocean, in Carteret's day, was a very different matter. He had no chronometer with which to ascertain Greenwich Mean Time and in the result the longitude he gave for the island was more than three degrees out, nearly 200 miles too far west.

The consequence was that anyone looking for this island and unaware of Carteret's error would be gravely misled. The difficulty was increased for Christian by the fact that he himself could not rely upon his own longitude. The *Bounty* carried a timepiece or chronometer, but only one, and nearly two years had elapsed since the timepiece had been checked and there was not a second chronometer on board with which to compare. Christian, therefore, could not be sure of the error and rate of his single chronometer. He would not know where he was when he thought he had arrived at the position given by Carteret, and he would not know that the island was nearly 200 miles to the west. In the circumstances, it was quite a feat of navigation on his part to find the island at all.[1]

*　　*　　*

One very important factor in the task of building up the British Empire at this time and of accurately defining 'places marked red on the map of the world' was the marine chronometer. The increasing range of ocean voyages and the ensuing difficulty experienced by navigators in fixing the position, not only of their ship but also of their discoveries, made a reliable method of determining the longitude of increasing importance and urgency. Latitude was not enough, although easily and accurately found. The longitude could be ascertained only by lunar observations and by account or dead (deduced) reckoning. Both were extremely unreliable and laborious. Longitude is time and the early navigators did not know the time to the degree of accuracy which was necessary, namely correct within a few seconds. As early as 1714, the English Government offered handsome money prizes for a method that would enable the navigator at sea to determine his longitude within an error of sixty miles, forty miles and thirty miles respectively. The rewards offered were £10,000, £15,000 and £20,000, very large sums in those days. Holland, Venice, France, Spain and other maritime powers also offered rewards, but the largest and most famous was that of England.

The reward remained on offer for fifty years, and it was not until 1765 that the great prize was finally won, only for its payment to be shamefully delayed. The problem that had baffled the great geniuses of the time, Newton, Halley, Huygens, Leibnitz and others was triumphantly solved by the invention of the marine chronometer, a marvellous timepiece, the unaided work of a Yorkshire carpenter, John Harrison. Harrison and his son had laboured long and lovingly over the construction of these highly original, intricate instruments. He built several with his own hands, being occupied six years in the construction of Number One, and two years in completing Number Two. Number Four was finished in 1759 and was subjected to most searching tests in a vessel on a voyage to Jamaica and back.

It was found that in the course of a five months' voyage under all conditions, of tropic heat, temperate cold, the rolling and pitching of the ship and other disturbances, Harrison's timekeeper lost fifteen seconds in five months, or an error of less than a tenth of a second per day. Here was an instrument with which the far-distant navigator in the Pacific Ocean could determine positions with accuracy.

[1] Captain Carteret's own Journal has recently been issued by the Hakluyt Society.

Harrison's Number One still 'tells the hours' at the National Maritime Museum and his name and his fame still survive among the navigators of today, as does the chronometer in the ships of today despite the increasing use of radar and radio.

When Bligh sailed forth in the *Bounty*, he was equipped with one of these chronometers, even then an historic timepiece since Cook had had it in the *Resolution* on his Second Voyage. Christian retained it on board after the mutiny and took it with him to Pitcairn Island.

Nineteen years later, Captain Mayhew Folger in the American trader *Topaz* of Boston sighted Pitcairn by chance, and landed there when Alexander Smith, the last of the *Bounty* mutineers alive, recounted his tale to Folger. On Folger's departure, Smith presented him with the *Bounty*'s chronometer, inscribed with the maker's name, Kendall, sufficient proof of both Smith's and Folger's stories.

The coming of the marine chronometer, which spread rapidly throughout the Royal Navy and the merchant ships, created a revolution in navigation. It coincided with the appearance upon the scene of the new school of navigators headed by Cook, and including Flinders, Bligh, Vancouver, Edwards and their contemporaries and those who came after them. The story of navigation may be divided into two periods, BC (Before the Chronometer) and AC (After the Chronometer).

Columbus, Magellan, Vasco da Gama, Drake, de Quiros, Tasman, Dampier and others, had sailed the seas without benefit of the Harrison timepiece. Cook was the first to employ it on long voyages around the world, and it was the principal aid which heralded the new science in contrast with the old haphazard 'by guess and by god' of the BC period.

Discovery and exploration were followed by surveys and charts. The accuracy of the charts depended chiefly upon the accuracy of the longitude. Accurate charts facilitated trading voyages. Trade followed the chronometer, which lessened losses at sea, reduced the length of voyages and marine insurance costs, and expanded the British Empire in all directions. All this was in great measure due to the marine timepiece of John Harrison.

A quarter of a century later, in 1814, Captain Sir Thomas Staines, commanding HMS *Briton*, reported to the Admiralty.

Briton, Valparaiso
18 Oct. 1814

I have the honour to inform you that on my passage from the Marquesas to this port I fell in with an island where none is laid down in the Admiralty, or other charts. . . . The island must undoubtedly be that called Pitcairn's, although erroneously laid down on the charts. . . .

In company with the *Briton* was HMS *Tagus*, commanded by Captain Pipon who wrote:

It is an extraordinary circumstance that chance & meer accident should have led us hither, for had we been aware that Pitcairn Island was near us, we should have avoided it, we considering ourselves nearly 200 miles from it when land was discovered, and we verily believed that in sight was some new discovery.

On the whole it seems perhaps that Captain Edwards was wise not to 'turn' his ship in search of Pitcairn and to steer instead for Tahiti.

Christian probably found the island by sailing east and west along the parallel of latitude given by Carteret until he at last sighted it. After all, Pitcairn is a conspicuous seamark, rising to 1,000 feet and visible for forty miles on a clear day from the masthead. But Christian might have sailed past it and missed it on a dark night, or in a rain squall.

Here at Pitcairn Island, the *Bounty* and her people found their last resting-place, not altogether a peaceful one.

But that is another story.

Chapter 6

The Brig *Mercury*

AFTER Christian had sailed away in the *Bounty* from Matavai Bay, the sixteen who remained settled down to the pleasant island life. They separated into groups, most if not all finding a native woman with whom to live. Some of them waited patiently for a ship to arrive from England, some of them began building a vessel in which they might leave the island, and some began to raise families. To their surprise, they heard from the islanders that there was another white man on the island, of whom strange tales were told.

While Christian and the *Bounty*'s people were making their second and prolonged attempt to settle down permanently on Tubuai, between 26 June and 16 September, unknown to them another British vessel had arrived and anchored in Matavai Bay. This was the brig *Mercury*, a fine, new copper-bottomed vessel of only 150 tons which had been built at Deptford Yard to the order of Captain J. H. Cox, who both owned and commanded her. Captain Cox was an enterprising individual who had become interested in the fur trade in Alaskan waters and had had the *Mercury* built in order that he might visit that region and investigate the fur trade at first hand. With him as a passenger and companion went Lieut. George Mortimer of the Royal Marines who, on his return to England, published a small volume describing the voyage.[1]

The *Mercury* sailed from Gravesend on 26 February 1789, bound for Alaska via Tahiti, and, as Captain Bligh did not reach England with news of the mutiny until 14 March 1790, Cox and Mortimer were not aware of it. On the day of the mutiny the *Mercury* was running down her easting in the Roaring Forties making for St Paul and Amsterdam Islands which they visited. Then Captain Cox visited Van Diemen's Land, after which he squared away for Tahiti where he anchored in Matavai Bay on 13 August 1789.

---

[1] This excessively rare volume does not seem to have been known to Sir Basil Thomson or to Rutter, but Dr G. Mackaness includes it in his Bibliography. Thomson refers to the *Mercury* as an American vessel and Rutter following Thomson does the same. She was, in fact, built and owned in Britain and sailed under the British flag.

On their way to Tahiti, they passed Tubuai, where the *Bounty* then lay. Mortimer notes: 'On 9th August, at 8 p.m., we passed within two miles of Tubuai and perceived several lights on shore. We fired two guns but night prevented us from seeing any of them.'

Had the *Mercury* passed Tubuai in daylight, Captain Cox might have seen the *Bounty* and decided to have a talk with her captain. This would have been an intriguing conversation, for Captain Cox, knowing naught of the mutiny, must have surmised that he was gazing at the *Bounty* while Captain Christian would have been hard put to it to explain.

On his arrival at Matavai, Captain Cox was informed by the natives who as usual swarmed on board that the *Bounty* under Captain Titreano (Fletcher Christian) had left Tahiti only fifteen days before the *Mercury* arrived, that is, about 28 July. We now know, however, that Christian had sailed from Tahiti on his return to Tubuai on 16 June, not fifteen but fifty-eight days before. One of the natives informed Mortimer that Bligh's chief officer, Titreano (Christian), had returned to Tahiti in the *Bounty* about two months after Captain Bligh had sailed and he (Christian) had told them that Bligh had been left on another island named Tootate.[1] Mortimer comments: 'Where Tootate could be, or who they meant by Titreano, we could not conjecture but I have not any doubt that the principal part of this strange relation is true.' (This account by Mortimer was, of course, made by him in his book after his return to England when he learned of the mutiny.)

This was the first that Cox and Mortimer had heard of the *Bounty* which had sailed from England fourteen months before them. Even if they knew of the departure of the Bread-Fruit expedition, they may have forgotten all about it, being fully preoccupied with their own ship then building at Deptford. In any case they had no personal interest in and probably no knowledge of Bligh and the *Bounty* and certainly the name of Christian would have meant little to them. But after Mortimer's return to England, everything became plain. The story of the *Bounty* was the sensation of the time. He went to the Admiralty and told them what he had heard while at Tahiti.

As a result of our visit to Otaheite, I was enabled to communicate such intelligence to the Admiralty respecting the probable destination of the mutineers of His Majesty's ship *Bounty* as it is hoped will enable Captain Edwards of the *Pandora*[2] to bring them to that condign punishment they so richly merit.

[1] This coincides with the story told to the natives by Christian. Tootate is presumably Aitutaki.

[2] Which had not then sailed on her mission.

While at Tahiti Mortimer was shown by the natives the grave of a white man whom they said was the *Bounty*'s surgeon. 'I have been informed, since my return to England, that he was the *Bounty*'s surgeon, Thomas Huggan, but the natives could not get nearer to a pronunciation of his name than Trono. They professed a great regard for him and for his skill in the healing art.' The surgeon, according to Bligh, was an alcoholic and died from the effects of hard drinking in a tropical climate.

Bligh related how he had sought permission from the chief Tinah and his father to bury the body on shore and took two men to dig the grave at the chosen spot, but found that the natives had already begun to dig it.

'Are we doing right?' asked Tinah. 'The sun rises there, and it sets there.' The idea that the grave should lie east and west I imagine they learned from the Spaniards as the captain of one of their ships was buried at Oetepeha in 1774.[1] Certain it is they had not the information from anybody belonging to our ship, for I believe we should not have thought of it. The grave however was marked out very exactly.

Mortimer also purchased from one of the islanders a native club.

He told me it had been brought from Tootate (Aitutaki) by one Titreano (Christian) and that he (Titreano) returned to Otaheite in the *Bounty* about two months after she had first sailed without Captain Bligh who was left at Tootate. He also told me that Capt. Bligh had had an engagement with the men of Tootate in which one of his people was killed with just such a club as I had purchased of him.[2]

The *Mercury* remained at anchor in Matavai Bay from 13 August until 2 September, a period of twenty days, during which there was frequent contact with the Tahitians and a visit was also made to the neighbouring island of Moorea.

On 2 September 1789, Captain Cox weighed and proceeded in the course of his voyage visiting[3] the Sandwich Islands and Hawaii *en route* to the fur trade in the north-west. Thence Captain Cox crossed the Pacific and arrived at Canton on 1 January 1790. From here, Mortimer took passage for England and on arrival home heard all about the mutiny in the *Bounty* and at once reported to the Admiralty what he had heard at Tahiti. This information, for what it was worth, was communicated to Captain

[1] This was Don Domingo de Boenechea, commanding the Spanish frigate *Aguila*, who died and was buried at Tahiti on 26 January 1775.

[2] Bligh lost a man (John Norton) at the island of Tofoa but this was after the mutiny and Norton was stoned to death, not clubbed.

[3] Sixteen days later, the *Bounty* arrived from Tubuai and anchored in Matavai Bay.

Edwards then fitting out the *Pandora*. But, since Mortimer had had no knowledge of or interest in Bligh and the *Bounty*, he had not troubled to collect all the information which he would have done had he known, and the highly garbled and inaccurate remarks volunteered by the natives, who themselves did not know of Bligh's troubles, conveyed little to him.

Some years later, in 1805, when Mortimer had been promoted from lieutenant to captain, he came into close personal contact with Bligh, being posted to HMS *Warrior*, commanded by Bligh who had been brought to a court martial by one of his lieutenants, John Frazier. Frazier alleged that Bligh had insulted and ill-treated him. Among the witnesses called was Mortimer, the captain of Marines.

Mortimer testified that Captain Bligh 'was frequently very violent and passionate and that his conduct was tyrannical and un-officer-like', but he went on to say that the Captain's conduct towards the Marine officers on board was 'polite and attentive'.[1]

Bligh evidently did not like Mortimer's evidence. He wrote to his patron, Sir Joseph Banks, after the court martial: 'The Capt. of Marines is Mortimer, who made that foolish voyage to the South Sea – as soon as his year of duty is up, I shall write to get rid of him.' The 'foolish voyage' had been made fifteen years before and it was not made by Mortimer, who was a passenger, but by the owner Captain J. H. Cox. The 'foolish' voyage was, in fact, a remarkable private enterprise involving a voyage round the world in a vessel of 150 tons. It included visits to St Paul and Amsterdam Islands in the Roaring Forties, and to Alaska in the far north, always in search of new trade opportunities by her enterprising and courageous owner and master.

And Mortimer himself should surely be commended rather than criticized for his readiness to make the voyage.

---

[1] Bligh was reprimanded by the Court and admonished to be more correct in his language.

Chapter 7

The Strange Case of J. Brown, A.B.

A CURIOUS incident occurred during the *Mercury*'s stay in Matavai Bay and is described by Mortimer: '15 August, 1789. At night, John Brown, one of our seamen, a desperate fellow, and who had before been guilty of several misdemeanours cut another sailor across the face with an old razor in a terrible manner for which he was immediately put in irons.'

While meditating in his cell on his troubles, Brown seems to have concluded that the best thing for him to do was get away from it all, and to ask Captain Cox to leave him behind at Tahiti when the *Mercury* sailed. Mortimer writes:

In the evening Otoo, His Majesty,[1] took his final leave of us and set off in his double canoe for Oparre, carrying with him Brown, the man who had been confined for wounding his messmate. It was Brown's desire to remain at Otaheite and we were glad of the opportunity to get rid of a troublesome fellow. Otoo seemed highly pleased at Brown being suffered to stay and promised to protect and take care of him.

Brown left the ship without showing the least regret at parting from his country-men or on taking leave of a single person on board. He seated himself in the canoe with all the assurance imaginable, telling the natives to hand down his hammock, etc.

Otoo requested Captain Cox to tell King George to send him a large ship with a great number of guns and men to be stationed in Matavai Bay, together with a quantity of scarlet and blue coats.

August 24. The captain received a letter from Brown in which he informed him that he was content with his situation and was well treated by the natives. He petitioned for a Bible, some carpenter's tools and a few other trifling articles which were sent to him, accompanied by a letter of good advice from the captain with regard to his future conduct and behaviour towards his new friends.

Among the articles Brown seemed most desirous of obtaining was a quantity of large nails, as he meant to build a stout boat.[2]

[1] Otoo was then hardly 'His Majesty' but at that time merely the local chieftain of Matavai who later became His Majesty King of Tahiti. See page 33.

[2] Perhaps John Brown had already discovered what his many predecessors had found out – that the price of love in Tahiti was one iron nail.

'The man whom Captain Cox left here, called Brown, had a son.' (Captain Bligh on his Second Voyage to Tahiti.)

He was an ingenious man and could turn his hand to anything so that I have no doubt he will make himself agreeable to the Otaheitians and be much caressed by them, especially as it will be out of his power to obtain any spirituous liquors to the drinking of which he was much addicted and which had an effect upon him nearly equal to madness.

From 2 September when the *Mercury* sailed away until 20 September when the *Bounty* arrived from Tubuai, Brown was the only white man at Tahiti. The Sixteen from the *Bounty* soon learned of the presence of Brown and that the *Mercury* had recently left the island. Brown himself asserted that he was not at all pleased when the Sixteen arrived and settled themselves in. He told Captain Edwards when he arrived in the *Pandora* that he had been under the necessity, for his own safety, 'to associate with the pirates, but he took the opportunity to leave them as soon as possible'.[1]

Surgeon Hamilton of the *Pandora* also had some remarks about Brown:

He was an Englishman that had been left on shore by an American vessel that had called here, for being troublesome on board but otherwise a keen, penetrating active fellow who rendered many eminent services, both in this expedition and the subsequent part of the voyage. He had lived upwards of twelve months among the natives, adopted perfectly their manners and customs, even to the eating of raw fish, and dipping his roast pork into a coconut shell of salt water, according to their manner, as substitute for salt. He likewise avoided all intercourse with the *Bounty*'s people, by which means necessity forced him to gain a pretty competent knowledge of their language; and from natural complexion he was much darker than any of the natives.

James Morrison, formerly bo'sun's mate of the *Bounty* and one of the Sixteen who remained at Tahiti, took rather a different view of John Brown:

According to his story he had been a Serjeant in the Portsmouth Division of Marines but being broke[2] had gone to India in the *Eurydice* frigate where he left her and stayed in the Country and was cook to Col. Bailly when he was taken by Hyder Ally into whose Service he entered and turning Musselman was made an officer; this Service he soon left and coming down to Fort St. George (Madras) soon found an opportunity, in company with some others, to seize on a small vessel loaded with Company's Goods which they carried off. He was afterwards taken and tried, but for want of evidence against him, he escaped punishment but was sent to England where he soon found the Country too hot for him and having made a voyage in H.M.S. *Pomona* he left her and got on board the Brig *Mercury* from which he put on shore in this Island.

---

[1] Edwards' report. [2] Disrated or discharged—not penniless.

When he was gone, Poeno produced a letter signed 'T. H. Cox' wherein the Vessell is called His Swedish Majesty's Armed Brig Gustavus IIIrd, and wherein he calls Brown an ingenious handy man when Sober but when Drunk a Dangerous fellow. This letter was brought to Poeno and this agrees with Brown's account, as he said she was bound to the Sandwich Islands and from thence to China. As Brown found this letter in Poeno's possession afterwards, he secured it himself, to prevent it from being of any further use in pointing out his Character which, according to his own account, was black enough.

Later on, in his Journal under date 6 November, Morrison notes:

Brown had been playing tricks with Ellison's cutlass at Attahooroo and had it taken from him by the natives and a scuffle ensued. We found on enquiry that Brown had been the Aggressor, we told him that he must endeavour to live peaceably and not bring himself into trouble, otherwise he must stand to the Consequences, and as he found we would not support him, he Contented himself for the present, and Poeno having given him a house and piece of Ground, he remained quiet in Matavai for some time, the Natives never troubling him as they supposed he was under our protection, though they knew he was a Stranger to us, and he often Used them very ill which on our Accounts they took no notice of and they allways allowed for His not understanding their language or Customs.

It seems, therefore, that Brown's account to Captain Edwards of how he had been under the necessity, for his own safety, to associate with the pirates and that he left them as soon as possible, directly contradicts Morrison's story that Brown was a nuisance and that they were glad to be rid of him.

Previous writers on the *Bounty-Pandora* story seemed to have overlooked the case of John Brown on Tahiti. Among the authorities on Captain Bligh and the mutiny and its aftermath is Owen Rutter. For twenty years he had made a detailed study of this subject which he had made his own. But in this detail of the movements of the *Mercury* he acknowledged that he was completely baffled. A glance at Mortimer's little book would have solved his problem. In one of his books[1] Owen Rutter has a footnote:

The Master of the American ship *Mercury* [she was not an American ship but a British brig] left Brown behind because he had had trouble with him. The presence of this man raises an interesting point. Hayward, one of the *Bounty*'s midshipmen in the boat with Bligh who returned to Tahiti in the *Pandora* with Captain Edwards [as a lieutenant] stated at the Court Martial on the mutineers: A European by the

[1] Rutter, *Court Martial of the* Bounty *Mutineers*, p. 116, footnote. Rutter, however, suggests as an afterthought the real answer to his question.

name of Brown had been left by a ship that had visited Otaheite since the departure of Bligh in the *Bounty*. . . .

Rutter comments:

The presence of this man Brown raises an interesting point. Hayward says the *Mercury* touched at Tahiti after Bligh had left. Yet the Admiralty had told Captain Edwards that he might get some useful information from Brown. Hamilton, the *Pandora*'s surgeon, says that Brown had been upwards of twelve months on Tahiti. If that is so, the *Mercury* must have arrived at Tahiti while the mutineers were there. Why, then did not Heywood and the others get a passage in her? How did the Admiralty learn of Brown's presence at Tahiti? These are questions the Editor confesses he has not been able to clear up satisfactorily.

As regards his first query, the answer is, of course, that the *Mercury* *arrived and sailed* during the absence of the *Bounty* at Tubuai. Nobody in the *Bounty* had the least idea of the *Mercury*'s existence, let alone her arrival at Tahiti, until the Sixteen returned to Tahiti to settle there and found Brown there. As Christian and his party remained less than twenty-four hours at Matavai Bay before sailing for Pitcairn, they may not have known of Brown at all.

In his Journal, James Morrison wrote:

Immediately on our landing, the islanders informed us that a vessel had been there lately and had left a man who they Call'd Browne who was then at Tyarraboo with Matte.[1]

As we heard they told strange storys of him, we wished to know what had been the true Cause of his Stay and therefore appointed Churchill and Millward to go to Tyarraboo & take some presents to Matte and at the same time to see who this man is . . .

They returned to Matavai 10th October bringing the Englishman who called himself Brown alias Bound., and said he had been left on shore from the Brig *Mercury*. T. H. Cox Esqr., Commander, of London. He said he had stayed at his own request, having had a dispute with some of his shipmates and cut one of them a Cross the Face with a knife, this and some other things which he related of himself was sufficient to give a very good idea of his Character and to put us on our Guard against one who appeared to be a dangerous kind of man. However we each gave him some addition to his Stock of Cloaths and he soon mustered as good a Stock as any of us had. He had got from Captain Cox an augur, some Gimbles, and a Plain which were the whole of his tools, though as he had no work to do, these were more than he had any occasion for.

He set out on 18th [October] with Burkitt to see Matte at Tyarraboo. . . .

[1] Matte was Morrison's name for Otoo, the Chief of the Matavai Bay district. Surgeon Hamilton refers to them as 'King Ottoo and his Queen Edea'.

The following chronological table will make these movements clear:

1787	..	23 Dec.	*Bounty* leaves England
1788	..	26 Oct.	*Bounty* arrives Tahiti
1789	..	26 Feb.	*Mercury* leaves England
		4 April	*Bounty* leaves Tahiti with bread-fruit
		28 April	The Mutiny
			Mercury en route to Van Diemen's Land
		25 May	Mutineers reach Tubuai
		6 June	Mutineers reach Tahiti
		16 June	Mutineers leave Tahiti for Tubuai
		26 June	Mutineers reach Tubuai
		9 Aug.	*Mercury* passes Tubuai in darkness
		13 Aug.	*Mercury* arrives Tahiti
		2 Sept.	*Mercury* leaves Tahiti (and Brown)
		16 Sept.	Mutineers leave Tubuai
		20 Sept.	Mutineers arrive Tahiti
		21 Sept.	Christian in *Bounty* sails for Pitcairn
1790	..	1 Jan.	*Mercury* arrives Canton
		14 March	Captain Bligh arrives back in England
		25 Oct.	Lieut. Mortimer arrives in England
		7 Nov.	*Pandora* leaves England
1791	..	23 March	*Pandora* arrives Tahiti and finds Brown there.

Morrison's friend or Tayo whom he names Matte was an important chief who enjoyed many names and titles confusing to the reader. Among his other names were Tinah, Tu, O Tu, and subsequently Pomare I. He was the paramount chief in the island when Captain Cook visited it. Since he resided in or near Matavai Bay, to all the Europeans whose ships anchored there he became well known and was generally regarded as the principal chief of the whole island. This led them to style him the 'King' and his wife Iddeah the 'Queen'.

Matte, Tinah or Tu gradually acquired a significant pre-eminence over his rivals for power by the fortuitous chance that his headquarters in the Matavai district became also the headquarters and principal rendezvous of all the European ships visiting the island. When the chief or king came on board in state it was Tu. When the European captains negotiated with the local king it was Tu to whom they went with their complaints and requests. Tu was the friend and Tayo of Captain Cook, Captain Bligh, Captain Edwards and of the bo'sun's mate, James Morrison. King Tu was the friend of King George III who sent him gifts through his naval commanders, the King Tu reciprocated, as one king to another.

Surgeon Hamilton records that when the *Pandora* was about to sail:

King Ottoo and his queen Edea came on board and were very importunate in their solicitations to Captain Edwards requesting him to take them to England with him. But the other chiefs remonstrated against his going as they were on the eve of a war. Notwithstanding that the King be a broad-shouldered strapping fellow, three sturdy stallions of *Cecisbeos* or lords-in-waiting are kept for the particular amusement of the Queen, when his majesty is in his cups. Yet the royal issue is always declared to be sprung from the immortal gods.

In course of time O Tu gradually established his ascendancy over the whole island and changed his style and title to Pomare I, King of Tahiti, thus founding a royal dynasty. The reigning queen Pomare IV died in 1872 after a troubled reign of fifty years and her son, Pomare V, was forced to cede his kingdom to France in 1880.

Chapter 8

And of J. Morrison

ONE of the Sixteen who preferred to remain on Tahiti rather than to accompany Christian to some unknown destination was the *Bounty*'s bo'sun's mate, James Morrison, aged thirty-one.

He had joined the navy as a youth, was a qualified Master Gunner for Third Rates and had passed an examination in elementary navigation, so that he was better qualified than his lowly station as a bo'sun's mate in the *Bounty* would indicate. He seems to have been a cut above his shipmates and Sir Basil Thomson said of him that he seems to have belonged to 'that objectionable class of seamen – the sea lawyer' but adduced no evidence in support, except that he kept a diary or journal. The name of James Morrison has been prominent in the *Bounty-Pandora* literature because he wrote a long, detailed, interesting account of the whole business, including the passage out in the *Bounty*, the mutiny, and the subsequent proceedings in the *Pandora*, in all of which he was an observant onlooker and actor.

This document, known as the *Journal of James Morrison*, presents a problem, however. The title, Journal or Diary, implies that it was a day-to-day record, written down at the time. Morrison is supposed to have kept a notebook or books both in the *Bounty*, during the mutiny, at Tubuai and Tahiti, and on the return passage to England.

It is claimed that he preserved these notebooks throughout all his adventures which included many desperate situations and that when he finally arrived back in England and was awaiting trial for mutiny he employed himself in writing up these notes into a consecutive narrative or Journal. This extended to 300 pages of foolscap, which he later handed over to his former shipmate Peter Heywood, from whom it passed to Heywood's stepdaughter, Lady Belcher. She was the authoress of *Mutineers of the 'Bounty'* in which she included long extracts from Morrison's Journal. On her death, the MS passed to the Rev. A. G. K. L'Estrange and on his death in 1915 it was presented to the Trustees of the Mitchell Library in N.S.W. who later gave permission to Owen Rutter to print it. Owen

Rutter considers that Morrison employed himself in writing up his 'Journal' *while he was awaiting trial* in Portsmouth.[1] Dr G. Mackaness thought that Morrison wrote up the complete story from his notes 'some time after the court martial'.

While he was in Portsmouth, Morrison was a closely guarded prisoner, under constant supervision, a mutineer likely soon to be hanged. In such circumstances it seems improbable that he would have been provided with pens, ink and 300 sheets of foolscap.

Was he quite free in his cell to write a considerable volume including severe criticisms of Captain Bligh at the very time when he was about to be tried for his life on a charge of mutiny against Captain Bligh? His complaints against Bligh refer to the severity of the discipline which, he says, led to discontents and murmurings, indeed to mutiny. Nor did he spare Captain Edwards. Surely Morrison would not have risked his life by writing such subversive matter in his cell at such a time. It seems highly improbable that the naval discipline of the day would have allowed Morrison to call for pen, ink and paper and with the knowledge and approval of the authorities sit calmly and openly recording his criticisms of his captains.

If one assumes that whatever notebook or diary Morrison kept was not in his possession when he finally arrived in England, what happened to it? When he was placed under arrest and in irons in the *Pandora*, he would have been searched and any notebooks taken from him, as was done in the case of Midshipman Peter Heywood. Why should Edwards seize Heywood's Diary and leave Morrison's? It was a strict Admiralty rule that journals, diaries, etc., kept on board such ships should be surrendered to the Admiralty on the vessel's return to England to prevent publication before the official account and to prevent disclosures of new discoveries etc., to foreign powers.

If, however, Morrison had not been able to preserve his notes or memoranda, how did he write up a complete and detailed narrative of all that happened, giving accurate dates and recording conversations several years afterwards? Considerable importance has been attached to the fact that Morrison's account and Captain Bligh's account closely coincide. It would be strange if they did not. Captain Bligh's *Narrative of the Mutiny in HMS Bounty* had been published in London before Christmas 1790 and became a best seller. James Morrison did not return to England until June 1792, in handcuffs, and was not freed until October 1792. Captain Bligh's book was the very 'note Book' he required to jog his memory, complete

[1] Rutter (ed.), *The Journal of James Morrison*.

with official facts and dates.[1] Morrison's Diary or Journal is neither. In my opinion, it is his version, written up several years after the events described, of Bligh's story of the mutiny. But it contains also a valuable and factual account of Morrison's adventures after the mutiny and a first-hand account of manners and customs of the Tahitians at that time.

Another clue to the origins of Morrison's *Journal* is afforded by a comparison between the entries in his *Journal* and those in Surgeon George Hamilton's *Voyage Round the World*.

This was published early in 1793, a few months after Morrison was reprieved and released. He would, therefore, not only have had Bligh's account of the mutiny, but Hamilton's account of the events in the *Pandora* and the subsequent boat voyage, in which he was involved. And also flatly to contradict the surgeon on occasion (see page 59 footnote).

[1] Midshipman Peter Heywood actually quoted Bligh's published *Narrative* at the court martial.

Chapter 9

The Schooner

THE Journal, however, was not James Morrison's only achievement. He was to a very considerable extent responsible for a spectacular feat in naval architecture, the design and construction of a thirty-ton schooner in which he purposed, somehow or other, to reach Batavia and thus return to England. That he should have entertained, however vaguely, such an idea seems to have been a strong point in favour of his consciousness of innocence regarding the mutiny. Those who had a sense of guilt felt, like Christian, that there was no hope for them. The Nine abandoned all idea of ever trying to return to England, whereas Morrison and some of the others, even while still in the *Bounty*, harboured a design of recovering control of the ship from Christian and his party.

In his Journal Morrison wrote: 'The behaviour of the officers on this occasion was dastardly beyond description, none of them even making the least attempt to rescue the ship which would have been effected had any attempt been made by one of them . . .' Nor did the allurements of the island life nor the charms of his island wife cause him to wish to spend the remainder of his life there. He was sufficiently intelligent and instructed to know that the nearest European outpost was the Dutch settlement at Coupang in Timor and he conceived the idea of constructing some type of vessel at Matavai Bay to sail thither. He confided these thoughts to Thomas McIntosh, one of the carpenter's crew, Charles Norman, carpenter's mate and Josiah Coleman, the armourer.

Morrison felt that it would be unwise for him to let everybody know that he intended to try to build a vessel in order to sail away from Tahiti but as everybody would see the vessel being built, he gave out that the schooner was intended, more or less, for pleasure trips around the island and to the neighbouring island of Moorea. Altogether ten of the Sixteen agreed to help in the task, foremost among them being the three skilled tradesmen, the armourer, the carpenter's mate and the cooper.

Their resources for the purpose were limited. When they had gone on shore from the *Bounty* they had taken with them a chest of carpenter's tools and some of the armourer's tools, together with a pig of iron to serve as an anvil, some bar iron, a grindstone, some old sails that Christian did not want and some pieces of old canvas.

At this time the Sixteen had separated themselves into congenial groups. Heywood went with Stewart to live on the land owned by Stewart's native wife, Peggy, the daughter of a leading chief; Coleman and Thompson were living with other islanders; Churchill and Skinner were with Skinner's father-in-law, and Muspratt, McIntosh, Norman, Hillbrant and the half-blind ship's fiddler Michael Byrne lived in nearby Oparra with the chief of that district. 'My friend Poeno', says Morrison, 'the Chief of the Matavai district invited me and Millward to live with them.'

They had landed from the *Bounty* on 20 September. By the end of October, having settled in and enjoyed all the pleasures of this tropic land, each with a 'wife' or girl friend, they were in the mood for some useful and definitive employment.

The first task in the building of the schooner involved the heavy labour of cutting planks from trees which had first to be felled. They had no saws at first but by an extraordinary stroke of luck, one was found. It had been a gift from Captain Cox of the *Mercury* to Iddeah, the wife of the chief of Matavai[1] and she at once agreed to give it to the boat-builders. 'It was quite new and unused and we were in great need of it,' wrote Morrison.

On 11 November they began felling trees and laying the blocks at the chosen spot, about half a mile from the beach. The next day the keel was laid. The heaviest labour was in transporting the logs and planks from the forest to the site, but by 15 March 1790, only four months after laying the keel, the frame was completed. An improvised forge and bellows was set up and Coleman completed most of the ironwork.

Morrison gives the following dimensions,

Keel	30 ft. 0 ins., the overall length on deck being 35 feet
Stern post	6 ft. 6 ins.
Stem	7 ft. 2 ins.
Beam	9 ft. 6 ins. amidships
Hold	5 ft. 0 ins.

By 1 July, the schooner, now named the *Resolution*, was ready for launching, but she was more than half a mile from the water. An army of Matavai people, totalling 400, was assembled for the purpose of dragging her down to the water, and she was successfully launched.

But they had no cordage to rig her and no canvas for sails. She was decked, caulked with resin fats and as large as a 'Gravesend boat'.

[1] Otoo or Tinah.

The problem of sails was surmounted by sewing together native mats and although this flimsy and makeshift arrangement gave the schooner a fair turn of speed, it limited the *Resolution* to short cruises around the island and across to the neighbouring island of Moorea. In the meantime she was hauled up and housed under a roof to protect her from sun and rain, the wet season being at hand. They had accomplished their aim, they had done all that was possible to create a vessel that would enable them to escape from what many of them regarded as their island prison, but the few short trips in the little vessel seemed to have forced them to the realization that without proper canvas sails and cordage, without adequate navigational instruments, without sufficient butts and casks for water storage, and with their limited knowledge of how to navigate, a prolonged voyage to a distant port such as Batavia was impracticable and would probably end in disaster. For the present it seemed that there was nothing else to do but to settle down again to their peaceful existence among their Tahitian friends.

There was George Stewart, aged twenty-two, a young man of good family, educated and trained, whom Christian had promoted to take charge of a watch in the *Bounty*. He was quite capable of navigating the little *Resolution* to Batavia, but there were no charts, no instruments and no incentive for him to uproot himself. For Stewart had become a regular and settled family man, the son-in-law of a prominent local chief. He had a nice house and garden, he had married a wife, Peggy, he had 'a dear little daughter'[1] and he was a keen gardener.

In *The Island*, Byron painted Stewart and Peggy in glamorous colours:

> There sat the gentle savage of the wild
> In growth a woman, though in years a child
> As childhood dates within our colder clime
> Where naught is ripened rapidly save crime
> The infant of an infant world as pure
> From Nature – lovely, warm and premature.
> With eyes that were a language and a spell
> A form like Aphrodite's in her shell.
> With all her loves around her on the deep
> Voluptuous as the first approach of sleep.

[1] Sir Basil Thomson states that this baby girl was 'the first half-caste born in Tahiti'. But on fewer than nineteen European vessels had visited Tahiti before the *Bounty*. This little daughter became a pet in Tahiti. When her mother Peggy died of a broken heart, the child was taken care of by her grandfather, a chief, and when the missionaries later arrived, they took charge of her. On his Second Voyage, Bligh noted: 'A fine child about twelve months old was brought to me today, the daughter of George Stewart, midshipman in the *Bounty*. It was a very pretty creature but had been so exposed to the sun as to be little fairer than an Otaheitian.'

Midshipman George Stewart RN was glamorized as:

> . . . the blue-eyed Northern child. . . .
> Say, what was he here?
> A blooming boy, a truant mutineer.
> The fair-haired Torquil, free as ocean's spray,
> The husband of the bride of Toobonai.
> By Neuha's side he sate, and watched the waters
> Neuha, the sun-flower of the island daughters. . . .

Then there was Peter Heywood, also a midshipman, a Manxman whose father and grandfather had been Deemsters, a youth with influential family connections who, at the time of the mutiny was only sixteen years of age though he was only five weeks short of seventeen.[1] Heywood was a scholarly type and he busied himself in compiling a vocabulary of the Tahitian tongue, while the others were employed about the schooner or in their own pursuits.

Into this peaceful scene there suddenly exploded a violent tragedy.

[1] Heywood's birth certificate gives 6 June 1772 as date of birth.

Chapter 10

Murder in Tahiti

AMONG the Sixteen on Tahiti were Charles Churchill and Matthew Thompson, ABs from the *Bounty*. It is rather surprising that these two should have decided in favour of remaining at Tahiti rather than follow their leader Christian to parts unknown. Churchill had been the *Bounty*'s master-at-arms or ship's corporal, a sort of ship's policeman, the one man in the crew who represented law and order, discipline and authority. In the event, he proved to be second only to Christian in the short, ruthless *coup d'état*. It was the policeman who was heard 'calling for a rope with which to tie up the captain'; it was he who had tried to desert while the *Bounty* lay in Matavai Bay collecting bread-fruit; it was he who had 'used a great deal of abusive language' to the captain at the mutiny and he who 'bore arms'. As for Thompson, he was armed with a cutlass and stood sentinel over the arms chest.

Churchill, together with Millward and Muspratt, had been flogged and ironed by Bligh for attempting to desert at Tahiti. Perhaps if they had waited until the night before the ship sailed, they would have had a better chance.

In the morning I read the Articles of War to the ship's company and punished the deserters as follows: Chas Churchill with 12 lashes, Muspratt and Millward with two dozen each, and remanded them back into irons for further punishment.

Wednesday 14 February. Punished Chas Churchill with 12 lashes, and Muspratt and Millward with two dozen each as their remaining part of their punishment for desertion and I directed them to be released from confinement.[1]

Although smarting from their wounds, and in irons, the three men either wrote, or got the clerk or somebody to write a letter to Captain Bligh:

On board the *Bounty* at Otaheite, January 26, 1789.
Sir,
    We should think ourselves inexcusible if we omitted taking this earliest opportunity of returning our thanks for your goodness in delivering us from a trial by

[1] Bligh's Log.

43

Court Martial, the fatal consequences of which are obvious; and although we cannot possibly lay any claim to so great a favour, yet we humbly beg you will be pleased to remit any further punishment, and we trust our future conduct will fully demonstrate our deep sense of your clemency, and our stedfast resolution to behave better hereafter. We are, etc.

C. CHURCHILL
WM. MUSPRATT
JOHN MILLWARD

To Captain Bligh

But the captain would not remit the further punishment. They brooded over their wrongs, although they had no wrongs since Bligh had saved them from a court martial on their return to England, desertion meaning almost certain death by hanging. Supposing Bligh had remitted the second instalment of lashes? Would his action have had any effect? The three men who were in Christian's watch might have challenged Christian, ranged themselves on the captain's side, thus averting the mutiny, and, as appeared in the upshot, preserved their own lives.

Looking back, it may be that the success of the mutiny in the *Bounty* was partly due to this incident and to Bligh's refusal to remit the second half of the punishment. Not that he is to be criticized on that account, or he would have been failing in his duty to carry out what was, in fact, a lenient punishment for a naval crime of the first magnitude.

Had Bligh sent for the three men and, after giving them a heart-to-heart talk, let them off, would he not have ranged them on his side and secured their loyalty on the day of the mutiny? If so, and if these three had reacted violently against Christian's action on the morning of the mutiny, their attitude might conceivably have nipped any mutiny by Christian in the bud. As it was, they took the lead with Christian.

*   *   *

At any rate, here they were settled comfortably down on Tahiti, two of them, Thompson and Churchill, living together, and having as their associate John Brown of the *Mercury*. Thompson, a man of forty, seems to have been a rather violent character, or else in his cups, when he ill-used a young girl who happened to belong to one of the leading families on the island. In revenge, her brother knocked him down and then fled. Thompson then seems to have gone berserk, for his next action was to fire his musket, killing a father and his child and breaking a woman's jaw. A little later a very bitter quarrel broke out between Thompson and Churchill. Churchill was shot dead by Thompson, the ball having passed below the shoulder through his body, entering at his back.

44

Morrison in his Journal says he went off to make enquiries when he heard that not only had Thompson shot Churchill but that Thompson himself was dead:

A man was called named Patirre who confessed that he had killed Thompson. The manner was this:—He was sorry for his friend's [Churchill's] death and was determined to be revenged on Thompson. Having got five or six more to join him, they went to Thompson's house and saluted him as Chief, and such like flattering stories until Patirre got between him and his arms, and knocked him down. The others whipped a short plank across his chest, and placed one on each end, while Patirre ran for a large stone with which he dashed his scull to pieces. They then cut off his head and buried the body.

Surgeon Hamilton writes:

The force of friendship among those good creatures will be more fully understood from the following circumstance. Churchill, the principal leader of the mutineers became the Tyo or friend of a great chief in the upper districts.[1] Some time after, the chief happening to die without issue his title and estate agreeable to their law from Tyoship devolved on Churchill who having some dispute with one Thompson of the *Bounty*, was shot by him. The natives immediately rose and revenged the death of Churchill their chief by killing Thompson, whose skull was afterwards shown to us, which bore evident marks of fracture.

And Captain Bligh, on his second visit to Tahiti, remarked:

A skull was kept with great care at this place, it being that of Thompson, one of the mutineers in the *Bounty*.

[1] Hardly a great chief. He was a mere boy named Natapua, heir apparent in the district of Taiarapu where he became principal chief on the death of his elder brother. But he himself died in 1790. He was succeeded in office by Churchill who had gained the youth's confidence and had been his Tyo. This corporal of Marines thus became an important personage in Tahiti for a short time until Thompson shot him.

Chapter 11

Rounding up the Pirates

ALTHOUGH the idea of sailing in the schooner *Resolution* from Tahiti to Coupang or to any other overseas port had been reluctantly abandoned by James Morrison, the stout little vessel, already successfully tried and tested, remained there before their eyes, well protected from the heavy rains. As soon as the rainy season was ended, they launched her again. There was not much else to keep the men occupied and the schooner afforded a ready means of transport to visit other parts of the island, on what were more or less pleasure and fishing trips. She was the wonder of the islanders and the pride of Morrison and his companions.

They launched her again in March and on 22 March 1791, a fatal day for the mutineers though they were not aware of it, sail was set and the *Resolution* glided out of Matavai Bay and headed south down the coast.

At this time the Fourteen now remaining on Tahiti were divided into three groups. The two midshipmen Stewart and Heywood kept themselves to themselves, busy with their own avocations at Matavai Bay. Richard Skinner, the *Bounty*'s barber, and servant of the Master, Fryer, also had a wife and a daughter at Matavai. Skinner must have had a bad conscience for in Fryer's cabin, at the time of the mutiny, were the keys of the arms chest, to which Skinner would have ready access. Bligh has a significant note in his private log book (Vol. 2) in which he records a conversation with Fryer during the open boat voyage. Bligh was not satisfied with the Master's inactivity during the short crisis of the mutiny.

The master's [Fryer's] cabbin was opposite to mine – he saw them [the mutineers] in my cabbin for our eyes met each other through his door window and he had a pair of ship's pistols loaded and ammunition in his cabbin. A firm resolution might have made a good use of them. These pistols I had ordered for the use of the officer of the watch since the 24th Jany, and they were at first kept in the binnacle but upon consideration that they might be stolen from thence, they were ever after kept in the master's cabbin. . . . He afterwards told me, on my questioning him, that he could find no body to act with – that by staying in the ship he hoped to have had it in his power to have retaken her; and that as to the pistols, he was so

46

flurried and surprised that he did not recollect he had them. His brother[1] said, on my enquiring how the keys of the arms chest came out of his cabbin, that the person who attended on him [Richard Skinner] had taken them away, which was certainly the case.

And certainly it was a strong case against Skinner should he be re-captured. Matavai Bay was a rather risky spot for a mutineer with a bad conscience, had Skinner known it, but here was his home where his wife and daughter lived, and this may have been the reason why he did not join the schooner's party.

Also at Matavai was Josiah Coleman, the armourer, ironworker and blacksmith who had forged all the ironwork for the schooner. He was one of the older steadier men, a man of forty who had an absolutely clean sheet.

He with Norman the carpenter's mate and McIntosh the carpenter's crew, had been expressly named by Bligh as 'detained contrary to their inclinations' and further as 'the most able men of the ship's company'.

While these four remained quietly absorbed in their avocations at Matavai Bay, the schooner sailed away with Morrison, Millward, Byrne, Norman, McIntosh, Hillbrant and Ellison on board to pay a visit to Burkitt, Sumner and Muspratt who had been living for some time at a spot further down the west coast known as Papara. The schooner arrived that evening and anchored there for the night, the night of 22 March 1791.

While the mutineers were enjoying themselves at Papara in the schooner, the *Pandora* was rounding the northern end of the island, feeling her way past Captain Cook's Point Venus and into the Bay of Matavai where she anchored shortly after dawn on the morning of 23 March 1791.

Even before she anchored, Josiah Coleman, the *Bounty*'s armourer, came on board with some natives, and from him Captain Edwards received an early account of the mutineers. Coleman was followed by the two midshipmen, Heywood and Stewart, and a little later came Richard Skinner. Thus within a few hours of his arrival, Edwards had safely on board four of the mutineers. To their somewhat naïve surprise, they were all four put in irons.

Edwards' commission from the Admiralty was to endeavour to seize and bring home in confinement the whole or as many of the mutineers or 'pirates' as he might be able to recover. He seems to have taken for granted that any member of the crew of the *Bounty* was *ipso facto* a mutineer, that all were to be regarded as guilty and all were to be treated equally.

He was not in a position to sort out the sheep from the goats as they

[1] Fryer's brother-in-law, an able seaman, Robert Tinkler who was also in the boat.

arrived on board. Only the court martial in England could do that, after a long investigation and the taking of evidence. Captain Bligh had been in England for six months before Edwards sailed, and Captain Bligh had very clearly indicated whom he regarded as 'villains' and those who had taken no part in the mutiny. For example, Bligh had officially noted that Norman, McIntosh and Coleman were 'detained against their Consent', but as soon as Coleman arrived on board he was put in irons.

Then there was the case of young Peter Heywood, a boy of sixteen when the mutiny occurred. The Heywood family and Mrs Bligh's family, the Bethams, were friends. Bligh had been a frequent visitor to the Heywood home and Peter was the favoured protégé of Bligh when he joined the *Bounty* aged fifteen. But something went wrong and after the mutiny, Bligh seems to have conceived a violent prejudice against the youth.

Shortly after his return to England, in a letter to Heywood's uncle, dated 26 March, he wrote:

With much concern I inform you that your nephew, Peter Heywood, is among the mutineers. His ingratitude to me is of the blackest dye for I was a father to him in every respect and he never once had an angry word from me through the whole course of the voyage, as his conduct always gave me much pleasure and satisfaction. I very much regret that so much baseness formed the character of a young man I had a real regard for, and it will give me much pleasure to hear that his friends can bear the loss of him without much concern.

A few days later Bligh received a letter from Peter's mother, to which he replied:

Madam,
I received your letter this day [2 April 1790 – less than three weeks after his return] and feel for you very much, being perfectly sensible of the extreme distress you must suffer from the conduct of your son Peter. His baseness is beyond all description but I hope you will endeavour to prevent the loss of him, heavy as the misfortune is, from afflicting you too severely. I imagine he is with the rest of the mutineers, returned to Otahiti.

I am, Madam, WM. BLIGH.

Captain Edwards must, therefore, have been heavily prejudiced against Midshipman Heywood before he left England. One of his officers in the *Pandora* was Lieut. Hayward, also a midshipman in the *Bounty*. He shared Bligh's opinion of his shipmate, for when Heywood arrived on board and seeing his old shipmate greeted him cordially, 'Lieutenant Hayward treated him with a sort of contemptuous look.' (Captain Edwards at the court martial.) Hayward's evidence at the court martial was in fact highly detrimental to Heywood, as was the other midshipman's, Hallett, who gave very damaging evidence against Heywood at the court martial saying that: 'Captain Bligh spoke to him, but what I did not hear, upon which he laughed, turned round and walked away.'

At any rate, innocent or no, all four were clapped into irons, and in the meantime strong parties from the *Pandora* were sent out to apprehend the remaining mutineers.

Heywood himself was quite shocked by his reception on board the *Pandora*. Some months later he had an opportunity of sending a letter to his mother, from Batavia, when homeward bound to stand his trial with the others:

Having learned from one of the natives that our former messmate, Mr. Hayward, now promoted to the rank of lieutenant was on board, we asked for him, supposing he might prove the assertions of our innocence. But he, (like all worldlings when raised a little in life) received us very coolly and pretended ignorance of our affairs. Appearances being so much against us, we were ordered to be put in irons and looked upon oh! infernal words! – as piratical villains.[1]

Having seen his ship safely moored in Matavai Bay in the best anchorage indicated on the charts by Captain Cook and Captain Bligh, and having swiftly absorbed the various reports of the 'pirates' given to him by Stewart, Heywood, Coleman and by several of the islanders, Captain Edwards acted with speed and decision. He had but just moored his ship in a strange harbour with which he was not previously acquainted, after a passage of five months in largely unknown waters. He was surrounded by a jabbering and excited crowd of islanders with conflicting reports and advice as to the whereabouts of the remaining 'pirates', but within four hours of anchoring he had put both his pinnace and launch into the water with strong landing parties under the command of two lieutenants, Corner and Hayward, and dispatched them in search of the schooner. He had three considerations in mind. First was the necessity of getting hold of the mutineers before they heard of his arrival and of taking them by surprise. Second was the desirability of having a native and reliable guide with local knowledge, and third was the fact that owing to the close bonds between the mutineers and the islanders, including several chiefs, these latter might aid and comfort the mutineers and try to defeat his measures to apprehend them. The native guide whom he sent with the two boats was Odidee. This remarkable young man had already voyaged with Cook.

[1] Tagart, *Memoir of Captain Peter Heywood*.

I had carried him from Ulietea in 1773 and brought him back to Tahiti in 1774 after he had visited the Friendly Islands, New Zealand, Easter Island, the Marqueses and been on board my ship in that extensive navigation about seven months.[1]

Odidee considered himself so much attached to the English that when Bligh was leaving Tahiti with the bread-fruit he made a strong claim to be taken to England on the ground of his long association with the great Cook. Now he was the only islander to be recruited by Edwards as guide for the capture of the mutineers.

Although Edwards hoped to take the mutineers by surprise, it was hardly possible for him to do so since the arrival of the *Pandora* at Matavai Bay was known to many of the islanders even before she arrived. Her track to Matavai Bay lay around the northern end of the island past Point Venus, and her slow approach on the evening of the previous day (22 March) must have been observed by the natives from the shore over a period of some hours, but not by the white men who were congregated down the west coast at Papara in the schooner. The unexpected arrival of a European ship would have been signalled throughout the island and the news would have spread immediately. It was indeed conveyed to the Ten at Papara as soon as the *Pandora* arrived. They learned also that two armed boats were on the way to capture them.

In his report to the Admiralty, Captain Edwards wrote:

The two boats were discovered by the pirates before they had arrived at the place (Papara) where these people had landed. They immediately embarked in their schooner and put to sea, and she was chased the remainder of the day by our boats, but, it blowing fresh, the schooner outsailed them, and the boats returned to the ship.

So ended the first day for Captain Edwards and for the mutineers.

When the two boats returned to the *Pandora* late that evening of the first day, they brought two passengers with them. One was Brown of the *Mercury*. As previously noted, Brown informed Captain Edwards that he had taken the first opportunity to leave the mutineers when they were about to embark in the schooner at Papara in a hurry and put to sea, and Captain Edwards readily accepted his services and entered him on the *Pandora*'s books.

With Brown there came one of the *Bounty*'s men, the blind fiddler Michael Byrne. Although nominally an able seaman, he had been recruited by Bligh for a specific duty.

Some time for relaxation and mirth is absolutely necessary and I have considered it so much so that after four o'clock the evening is laid aside for their

[1] Cook's Third Voyage.

amusement and dancing. I had great difficulty before I left England to get a man to play the violin and I preferred at last to take one two-thirds blind than come without one.

Byrne was very much handicapped by this blindness and he suffered from the nervous fear that his companions on Tahiti might abandon him, and that he would be left alone unable to find his way about. Suffering from this severe disability, it was clear that he could hardly have been prominent in the mutiny. Nevertheless he was at once put in irons by Captain Edwards along with the others.

From these four prisoners and from the islanders, Edwards was in possession of all the facts of the situation – that sixteen of the *Bounty*'s people had remained at Tahiti: that two of them, Churchill and Thompson, were dead, that nine were somewhere on the coast in a schooner that they had built which, together with the five now in his hands, made up the total of sixteen.

Chapter 12

The Pirates' Dilemma

THE Nine still at large in the schooner were faced with an alarming problem, and placed in a sharp dilemma. They simply did not know what to do. Morrison says that they all 'agreed to avoid seeing the *Pandora*'s two boats', but what purpose would be filled by 'avoid seeing' the two boats in hot pursuit of them is not apparent. He goes on to say that they put to sea as soon as they heard of the *Pandora*'s arrival, hoping by keeping out of sight of the boats, to reach the *Pandora* and to surrender to Captain Edwards of their own accord. This in the belief that by so doing they would receive better treatment, and possibly a better hearing at the inevitable court martial than if they were captured and brought on board as prisoners.

However, this idea of sailing to Matavai Bay and of going on board the ship as innocent men who were delighted to see the *Pandora* and to be welcomed on board by the gratified and hospitable captain was abandoned. For want of any other plan, and to replenish their food and water, the Nine returned to Papara, where the schooner was anchored, and they went on shore.

Captain Edwards in the meantime had been busy organizing his intelligence which included a network of news from the local chiefs. 'Early in the morning of March 27, I had information that the pirates were returning with the schooner to Papara and that they were landed and retiring to the mountains, to endeavour to conceal themselves.'

This news was fairly accurate, and Edwards at once sent Lieut. Corner with twenty-six men in the launch to apprehend them, and the next morning (28 March) he sent Lieut. Hayward with a strong armed party in the ship's pinnace to reinforce Corner.

Meanwhile the dilemma of the Nine remained unresolved. To go or to stay? To flee or to surrender?

One unseen influence was at work which prompted six of the Nine to come to a decision. The affairs of Tahiti at this time were disturbed by the rival claims of two chieftains – Otoo the chief of Matavai district, and Tamarie, one of the reigning dynasty of Tahiti.[1] Edwards writes:

I found the Otoo ready to furnish me with guides and to give me any other assistance in his power, but he had very little authority or influence in that part of the island where the pirates had taken refuge, and even his right to the sovereignty of the eastern part of the island had recently been disputed by Tamarie, one of the royal family. Under these circumstances, I conceived the taking (seizure) of the Otoo and the other chiefs attached to his interest into custody would alarm the faithful part of his subjects and operate to our disadvantage.

I therefore satisfied myself with the assistance he offered and had in his power to give me, and I found means at different times to send presents to Tamarie (and invited him to come on board, which he promised to do, but never fulfilled his promise) and convinced him I had it in my power to lay his country in waste, which I imagined would be sufficient at least to make him withhold that support he hitherto, through policy, had occasionally given to the pirates, in order to draw them to his interest and to strengthen his own party against the Otoo.

I probably might have had it in my power to have taken and secured the person of Tamarie, but I was apprehensive that such an attempt might irritate the natives attached to his interest and induce them to act hostilely against our party [meaning the *Pandora*'s two boat parties] at a time when the ship was at too great a distance to afford them timely and necessary assistance in case of such an event, and I adopted the milder method for that reason, and from a persuasion that our business could be brought to a conclusion at less risk and in less time by that means.

Like many other naval officers in command of a detached ship, Captain Edwards found himself becoming involved in the domestic affairs of the community, and wisely refrained from taking sides. But the refusal or disinclination of Tamarie to visit the *Pandora* seems to suggest his suspicions of Captain Edwards' intentions, and confirm that Tamarie was convinced that at Matavai, Edwards had ranged himself on the side of his rival Otoo, Chief of Matavai.

This view is confirmed by the action of the Six, who now, relying on the promised protection of Tamarie, took the final step of fleeing inland to the mountains to seek that protection, leaving the Three – Morrison, Norman and Ellison – to their own devices in the schooner, off Papara.

Morrison's state of mind at this crisis in his life can be only conjectured. His consciousness of his innocence had been compromised and weakened already by his dilly-dally tactics. The mere fact that he had seen the *Pandora*'s boats when they were in active pursuit of him, his companions and the schooner proclaimed him a fugitive from justice. He was, in a

[1] Variously spelt Tamarie (by Edwards), Tommaree and Pomare, the latter being the generally accepted name.

sense, the leader of the Nine, the best-educated, the most skilled, the progenitor of the schooner, and her captain. And he had led their flight from justice. Now, as he sat there reflecting on his position, it must have dawned upon him that the game was up. Already he had too much to explain away. What should he do now? He could follow the Six into the mountains; he and Norman and Ellison could sail away, somewhere, anywhere – into the blue, like Christian.

There were plenty of other islands and at a pinch three of them could handle the thirty-foot schooner. But the hue and cry was on. He was now a hunted man, and innocent men sometimes run away when they know the police are looking for them. Morrison didn't run away. He decided to leave the schooner where she was anchored, and to walk back along the beach, en route to Matavai some twenty-five miles to the northwards. He told the other two, Norman and Ellison, what he intended. They agreed and joined him.

Norman, in point of fact, need never have left Matavai with the other pirates and gone off in the schooner. He had an absolutely clean sheet and his innocence was never in doubt – not even in Captain Bligh's mind. He merely spoiled his clean sheet by going off in the schooner and by being one of those chased by the *Pandora*'s boats.

By one of life's little ironies, while Norman sat there on the deck of the schooner off far-distant Papara, gloomily contemplating his fate, on that very day a year previously, Captain Bligh was writing a letter to his brother.

No 4 Broad Street, St. George's East, London
March 26, 1790

Your unfortunate Brother, Charles Norman was Carpenter's Mate with me and was kept in the Ship against his will, and I have recommended him to Mercy – his friends may therefore be easy in the Minds on his account as it is most likely he will return by the first ship that comes from Otaheite. He was in very good health.

I am Your

WM. BLIGH

I only received your letter today.

There was, too, another document also signed by Captain Bligh which cleared Norman. He was one of the three, Norman, McIntosh and Coleman, whom Bligh had certified as 'being detained against their consent'.

Finally, Norman, the carpenter's mate, had an overwhelming incentive to go aboard the *Pandora* and to return to England. He had a wife and child awaiting him.

And Ellison, the boy Tom Ellison 'about fifteen years of age'. He was in the company of two men twice as old as he. It is no wonder therefore that he abided by their decision to give themselves up. At the court martial, after giving his account of the mutiny, Ellison concluded:

This, honourable Gentlemen of the Court, is the reale Truth of all I know about this unhappy affair and I hope your honour will take my Inexpearnce'd Youth into Consideration, as I never did or ment any harm to anyone, much more to my Commander to whose Care I was recommended by Mr. Camble (Campbell) a west India merchant in whose emply Captn. Bligh has sailed as commander in the *Britania* and *Lynx* both his ships. On account of this recommendation, Captn. Bligh took great pains with me and spoke to Mr. Samule (Samuel) his Clark to teach me Writing and Arithmetick and I believe would have taught me further had not this happened. I must have been very Ingreatfull if I had in any respect assisted in this Unhappy Affair agains my Commander and Benefactor, so I hope, honourable Gentlemen, you'll be so kind to take my Case into Consideration as I was no more than between Sixteen and Seventeen Years of age when this of done.

Honourable Gentlemen, I leave myself at the Clemency and Mercy of this Honourable Court

THOMAS ELLISON.

The honourable gentlemen were not impressed by the teenager's plea, found the charge proved against him and sentenced him to death by being hanged by the neck.

Chapter 13

The Pirates Surrender

HAVING concluded their reflections on their sad predicament, the two older men and the boy set out on the long march, perhaps their last march to the *Pandora*. Matavai was twenty-five miles away and they kept to the beach, trudging along. For some reason or other, the trio seemed to have walked late into the night for after covering about twelve miles from Papara, it then being about two o'clock in the morning, they came unexpectedly upon a ship's boat at anchor just off the beach. It was crowded with sleeping men. According to Morrison there was not even a sentry on watch, and he waded on board and awakened the officer in charge, Lieut. Corner, in command of the *Pandora*'s launch on its second journey down to Papara to capture the pirates.

They surrendered to the lieutenant and told him that the schooner was still at anchor off Papara. The officer, taking eighteen of his men, set off along the track to Papara, leaving seven of the boat's party and the prisoners in charge of Mr Richards, the master's mate. Shortly after another of the *Pandora*'s boats appeared coming down from the north. This was Lieut. Hayward in the ship's pinnace whom Edwards had dispatched to reinforce Corner. On his arrival, Hayward instructed Richards to bind the prisoners' hands and to return to the ship with them, while he himself proceeded in the pinnace to Papara. That afternoon, Richards reached the *Pandora* with his three prisoners who were at once placed in irons with an armed guard over them.[1] Edwards now had eight of the pirates safely in his hands.

There remained the Six who had fled inland to the mountains; all were able seamen:

[1] All this time, of course, we are told, Morrison presumably preserved his Journal, writing it up each day, possibly with a home-made quill pen and ink obtained from native dyes and fine sand wherewith to dry it. Doubtless as he trudged along the beach, his second thoughts were centred on the safety of his Journal. So, too, with his arrival on board when he was put in irons and locked up. Captain Edwards may or may not have had the pirates searched, but whether he was searched or not, Morrison was still able to write down daily a detailed record of the day's events, manacled or not.

William Muspratt	30
Thomas Burkitt	26
John Millward	30
Henry Hillbrant	28
John Sumner	28 and
Thomas McIntosh	28.

Not only were they able-bodied seamen, but some were skilled trades-men, Hillbrant being a cooper and Muspratt having served in the *Bounty* as Bligh's personal steward. He was one of the three who had attempted to desert while the *Bounty* was lying in Matavai Bay collecting bread-fruit. As Bligh's own personal cabin steward, he and the captain must have been on fairly intimate terms. Nevertheless, he tried to run away and when recaptured Bligh ordered him to receive four dozen lashes and to be ironed for a whole month, with the other two.

By all accounts, Burkitt was active in the mutiny and all the witnesses said he was armed. Bligh said he was one of those who came into his cabin which was confirmed by Lieut. Hayward and by the *Bounty*'s master, Fryer.

The case against Millward was strong since both Hayward and Hallett testified they had seen him armed. Millward's defence was that he was dragged in by Churchill who had forced a musket on him, but the master, Fryer, deposed that Millward had cocked his musket at him.

Sumner and Hillbrant did not survive to stand their trial.

These five were guilty men and no doubt were highly conscious of their guilt. Even if their consciences did not accuse them, they must have realized that, once they were captured, their end was certain. Their action in fleeing from the schooner and retreating into the interior, seeking aid and comfort from the islanders, indicates very clearly their state of mind. And yet, what could they have been thinking? Their case seemed hopeless. Here was Captain Edwards with a ship's company of 150 men, several large boats, unlimited arms and ample time in which to hunt them down and bring them back alive. The very fact that they had taken to the mountains to evade capture must have counted heavily, if not decisively, against them. Most if not all of the others had made great play of voluntarily surrendering themselves, conceiving that such action would tell heavily in their behalf. The five desperadoes took to the hills as if to resist capture to the last.

So much for the Five.

But what of Thomas McIntosh, the sixth and last in this group? What was he doing in that gallery? Like Norman and Coleman, his innocence was never in serious doubt. Bligh himself had testified in his defence – 'detained against his Consent'. And then there was his mother, Mrs Tosh, who held a valuable document on her son's behalf.

Mrs. Tosh

Your son who went by the name of McIntosh is on board the 'Bounty' in the South Sea – I was informed he remained on board contrary to his inclination, and therefore have recommended him to Mercy in case they should be taken. You may not expect to hear anything of him untill the *Pandora* returns which will be 18 months or two years.

I am

Your very Hmble. Servt.

London
Oct. 16th. 1790

WM. BLIGH

Apart from any question of his innocence or guilt, there was a strong motive no doubt influencing McIntosh to make one last effort to escape. He had acquired a young Tahitian bride and a child had been born to them quite recently. Until the arrival of the *Pandora*, McIntosh had been existing in an atmosphere of almost complete earthly happiness. The island, the bride, the baby – what more could he wish for? No wonder, innocent or guilty, that he made one last hopeless effort to escape.

As for his companions, they had some time earlier taken an important decision while still at Tubuai Island to return to Tahiti in the *Bounty*, to take their equal share, man for man, of the ship's stores and to settle down, peaceably and comfortably to the idyllic life of the island until. . . .

Until the expected ship from England arrived to take them back to England.

Now the expected ship had come and merely awaited their arrival on board. And yet they fled from her! How bitterly they must have regretted that they had not gone off with Christian, destination unknown.

* * *

The final preparations for their capture were now completed. Edwards had organized his tactical dispositions for securing them. He had won over the chief Pomare (Tamarie), says Surgeon Hamilton,

by sending him very liberal presents which effectually brought him over to our interest. The mutineers were now cut off from every hope of resource; the natives were harassing them behind and Lieut. Hayward and his party were advancing in front; under cover of night they (the mutineers) had taken shelter in a hut in the woods.

Hayward and his party had landed at Papara and were heading north through the jungle, while Lieut. Corner and a strong party from the ship were moving down from the northwards. He was accompanied by a large party of islanders, now openly and freely collaborating with the *Pandora*'s people under orders from the Big Chief, Tamarie, who had been so satisfactorily bribed by Edwards to this end.

And here John Brown of the *Mercury* reappears. Apparently detailed, or permitted, by Captain Edwards to accompany Hayward in the launch party for Papara, he was in the forefront of the search for the mutineers.

When one of the islanders informed Hayward that they had taken refuge in a hut in the woods, Brown volunteered to go forward and confirm the report.

According to Surgeon Hamilton 'he crept up to the hut where they were asleep, and distinguished them from natives by feeling their toes; as people unaccustomed to wear shoes are easily discovered from the spread of their toes'.[1]

At dawn, Hayward prepared for the assault, assuming that he would be met by six armed and desperate men who would fight to the last man. There was, however, no fight left in them. They surrendered without a shot being fired. Their hands were tied behind their backs, and they were marched back to Papara and taken back to the *Pandora*, where they were at once put in irons.

[1] The fact that Morrison had the advantage of reading Surgeon Hamilton's book when writing up his own Journal is shown by many signs. For example, Morrison wrote: 'Though they go bare-footed, their feet do not spread like the inhabitants of Africa and other hot Climates.'

Chapter 14

Pandora's Box

CAPTAIN EDWARDS had now completed his 'police mission' so far as lay in his power. Within a very short time he had secured the whole of the mutineers on Tahiti without losing a man. He had cultivated and cemented good relations with both the rival chiefs, Otoo and Tamarie; the master of the *Pandora*, George Passmore, had surveyed and made a detailed plan of Matavai Bay, and a prodigious number of goats, fowls, fruits and vegetables had been brought on board by the islanders. The crew of the *Pandora* had been kept busily occupied in caulking, watering, wooding and re-rigging the ship, and Morrison's schooner had been brought alongside, equipped with canvas sails, and put in commission as HMS *Resolution*. Edwards placed the master's mate, Mr Oliver, in command of her, assisted by Renouard, a midshipman, James Dodd a quartermaster and six Marine privates. He thought she would be a valuable tender to his ship in covering his boats in his further search for the *Bounty* and in reconnoitring the passages through the reef leading to Endeavour Strait.

Finally, the accommodation for the fourteen mutineers was now completed and HMS *Pandora* was in all respects ready for sea.

Captain Bligh had lingered at Tahiti for six months. Captain Edwards had completed his business in six weeks.

One of Captain Edwards' immediate problems, now that he had fourteen mutineers on board, was where to house them. His ship was already overcrowded with his complement of 160 and, according to Surgeon Hamilton

Our officers here, as at Rio Janeiro showed the most manly and philanthropic disposition by giving up their cabins and sacrificing every comfort and convenience for the good of mankind in accomodating boxes with plants of the bread fruit tree that the laudable intentions of government might not be frustrated from the loss of his majesty's ship *Bounty*.

Nor had the Admiralty, when the *Pandora* was being equipped for the voyage, fitted up any prison or cells in the ship for the prisoners' accommodation. They could be incarcerated either above or below decks and Edwards decided for above decks.

A prison was built for their acomodation on the quarter deck that they might be secure and apart from our ship's company; and that it might have every advantage of a free circulation of air which rendered it the most desirable place in the ship.... Orders were likewise given that they should be victualled in every respect the same as the ship's company, both in meat, liquor and all the extra indulgencies with which we were so liberally supplied, notwithstanding the established laws of the service which restricts prisoners to two-thirds allowance; but Captain Edwards very humanely commiserated with their unhappy and inevitable length of confinement.

This is the ship's surgeon's account of the notorious Cage or 'Pandora's Box' in which the mutineers were confined.

Captain Edwards merely stated in his Report to the Admiralty:

I put the pirates in the round house which I built at the after part of the quarter deck for their more effectual security, airy and healthy situation and to separate them from and to prevent their having any communication with, or to crowd and incommode the ship's company.

All of which seems to be a very sufficient justification for the Cage. Except for one serious objection. It was far too small, eleven feet by eighteen feet, to accommodate fourteen men.

Edwards would not let them out of it, not even in ones or twos for exercise and the calls of nature. Probably there was some excuse for this while the ship was still at anchor in Matavai Bay, but once at sea there would have been little or no risk in letting the men out for much needed exercise and other purposes.

The official story as conveyed in the reports of the Captain and the Surgeon gives no idea of the horrors of the Cage as told by two of the inmates, Morrison and Heywood.

They were not, of course, entirely detached observers. They were both men with a grievance of which nobody took much notice though their evidence must be accepted as giving part if not all of the facts.

Morrison wrote:

When the poop or roundhouse was finished, we were conveyed into it and put in irons as before. This place we stiled Pandora's Box, the entrance being a scuttle on the top, of 18 or 20 inches square, secured by a bolt on the top thro' the coamings; two scuttles of nine inches square in the bulkhead for air, with iron grates and the stern ports barrd inside and out with iron. The centrys were placed on the top, while the midshipman walked across by the bulkhead. The length of this box was 11 feet upon deck, and 18 wide at the bulkhead. No person was suffered to speak to us but the master-at-arms, and his orders were not to speak to us on any score but that of our provisions. The heat of the place when it was calm was so intense that the sweat frequently ran to the scuppers, and produced maggots in a short time, the hammocks being dirty when we got them we found stored with vermin of another kind which we had no method of erradicating but by lying on the plank; and tho' our friends would have supplied us with plenty of cloth, they were not permitted to do it, and our only remedy was to lay naked; these trouble-some neighbours and the two necessary tubbs which were kept in the place helped to render our situation truly disagreeable. . . .

Later on, when the *Pandora* was at sea, Morrison thus described conditions in the Cage:

Our miserable situation soon brought sickness on among us and the Surgeon (Mr. Hambleton) a very humane gentleman gave us all the assistance in his power but at the same time informed us that it was out of his power to be of any service to us in our present circumstances; however, between him and the Second Lieutenant [Corner] a copper kettle was provided to boil our cocoa in which was served with sugar in lieu of butter and cheese – and this, with the Divine providence, kept us alive. As the place was washed twice a week, we were washed with it, there being no room to shift us from place to place and we had no other alternative but standing up till the deck dried (which we could but very badly do when the ship had any motion) or lying down in the wet, and when the roughness of the weather gave the ship any motion, we were not able to keep ourselves fast, to remedy which we were threatened to be stapled down by the Captain, but Mr. Cornor gave us some short boards to check ourselves with, which he made the carpenters secure, and thereby prevented us from maiming each other and our-selves.

The gist of this second passage from Morrison is that it was all very uncomfortable and disagreeable in 'Pandora's Cage'. No doubt it was. It was also very uncomfortable and disagreeable for Captain Bligh and his party during their boat voyage. It was equally uncomfortable and dis-agreeable for all foremast hands and all apprentices in all sailing ships in all fo'c'sles and half-decks throughout the nineteenth and well into the twentieth century. 'Pandora's Box' was not much worse than the numerous typical half-decks inhabited by apprentices down to the First World War.

Oh yes, everything will be all right [in the half-deck] especially when we get down off the Horn and the dingy half-deck will be awash most of the time with icy water . . . with the ship working and green seas on deck and the water lashing about the floor, washing out the lower bunks, bed and bedding, and soaking every stitch of the clothing that we had fondly hoped would keep us moderately dry in the next bitter night watch.

And when the ill-hinged door swings to, and a rush of water and a blast of icy wind chills us to the marrow, it needs but a raucous shout from without to crown the summit of our misery: 'Out there, the watch! Turn out, damn ye!'[1]

Sir David Bone's description of life in the half-deck is merely a description of the normal life of all apprentices, youths in their 'teens – nothing at all to write home about.

In any case, what did Mr Morrison expect?

Surgeon Hamilton says the roundhouse was built partly out of consideration for the prisoners themselves in order to spare them prolonged imprisonment below in the tropics, and that although they were entitled to only two-third rations, Captain Edwards rationed them exactly the same as the crew.

If the conditions were so bad, how was it that not one of the fourteen was sufficiently ill to be transferred to the sick bay? Why did no one die, and how did the gently nurtured boys (Heywood, Stewart) survive these horrors? Surgeon Hamilton's principal duty was to keep a strict watch on their health and to bring them home alive. Had their continued existence been endangered by the conditions in 'Pandora's Box', a word from the surgeon to the captain would have been sufficient, though what Captain Edwards could have done is not easy to see. He could certainly have let them out for much needed exercise, but he was obsessed by the fear that they might contaminate the crew. These men were expert mutineers, skilled in the business. The *Bounty* had been a quiet take-over, conducted swiftly, silently and without a trace of violence. One moment the captain was in command – the next moment the chief mutineer. Christian had merely to dissemble his love for Bligh and then kick him firmly downstairs. It had been uncommonly easy, dangerously easy. Now Captain Edwards had fourteen of these 'pirates' on his hands in an overcrowded ship which was about to leave an island paradise where all hands had had a too scanty taste of honey. The attractions of this island magnet seemed to be infinite not only to the Fourteen, but to Surgeon Hamilton and the ship's company.

Although on the one hand, the visit of the *Pandora* to Matavai Bay had been an unqualified success, on the other there were many scenes of grief and woe. Every one of the fourteen prisoners, except perhaps young

[1] Bone, *The Brassbounder.*

63

Heywood, had established intimate relations with the island women, and most of these 'wives' had had children by the mutineers. The women were inconsolable at the near prospect of seeing their husbands for the last time – for ever.

The prisoners' wives visited the ship daily and brought their children who were permitted to be carried to their unhappy fathers. To see the poor captives in irons, weeping over their tender offspring was too moving a scene for any feeling heart. Their wives brought them ample supplies of every delicacy that the country afforded, while we lay there, and behaved with the greatest fidelity and affection to them.

The ship was filled with cocoa-nuts and fruit, as many pigs, goats and fowls as the decks and boats would hold. The dismal day of our departure now arrived. King Otoo and his queen Edea came on board and were very importunate in their solicitations to Capt. Edwards requesting him to take them to England with him. Aeredy the Concubine likewise requested the same favour but she more generously begged that they might all three go together. But Oripai, the king's brother and the other chiefs remonstrated against his going as they were on the eve of a war.

This I believe was the first time that an Englishman got up his anchor, at the remotest part of the globe with a heavy heart to go home to his own country.

Every canoe almost in the island was hovering round the ship, and they began to mourn as is customary for the death of a near relation. They bared their bodies, cut their heads with shells and smeared their breasts and shoulders with the warm blood as it streamed down. Otoo now took leave of us and with the tears trickling down his cheeks begged to be remembered to King George. With a pleasant breeze and our small consort in company we set sail.

It was the missionaries who, some years later, gave publicity to the sad end of Peggy, the beautiful young girl with whom Stewart had at once fallen head over heels in love and who reciprocated his passion for her. She was the daughter of a chief and he had provided a house and grounds for the young couple where they lived an idyllic existence until the arrival of the *Pandora* put a short, sharp and sudden end to it.

Frantic with grief, the girl flew with her infant in a canoe to the arms of her husband. The interview was so affecting and afflicting that the officers on board were overwhelmed with anguish and Stewart, unable to bear the heartrending scene begged that she might not be admitted on board again. She was separated from him by violence and conveyed on shore in a state of despair and grief too big for utterance. . . .[1]

[1] Wilson, *A Missionary Voyage to the Southern Pacific in the ship* Duff.

Morrison, himself in manacles, averred:

During the time we staid, the weomen with whom we had cohabited on the island came frequently under the stern (bringing their children of which there were 6 born, four girls and two boys, and several of the weomen big with child) cutting their heads till the blood discolloured the water about them, but they were always driven away by the Captn's orders and none of them sufferd to come near the ship.

Before he sailed and while the Cage was still being built, Edwards was privily informed by one of the chiefs of a conspiracy among the natives to cut the *Pandora*'s cables. One of the drawbacks of the anchorage at Matavai Bay is that fierce gales occasionally sweep in from the north-west converting the beach into a dangerous lee shore with a very high surf.[1] The plot apparently was to take advantage of the onset of such a gale, to sever the ship's rope cables in the hope that she would thereby be driven ashore. In the confusion, the Fourteen were to be rescued and conveyed to a hiding-place while Edwards and his crew were fully engaged in desperate efforts to refloat the vessel, a task probably beyond their powers.

Many of the prisoners were married to chiefs' daughters and Edwards was well aware of the influential backing behind such a plot. Had it been attempted and succeeded, the *Pandora* would probably have never been refloated with the facilities available, and the expedition would have been a total failure. Nor could the captain ignore the suspicion that his own men, attracted by the lure of the island life, would have been quite happy to remain there indefinitely.

A ceaseless watch was kept on the cables, sentries were posted throughout the night and Edwards kept his prisoners securely locked up and cut off from any communication with anybody.

But once he was clear away at sea, with the ship under sea discipline and routine, the risk of island plots vanished.

Then he might well have freed the prisoners from their manacles, at least during daylight, and allowed them out for an hour or two. Two sentries and a midshipman were on guard over them all the time, and he had brought his ship's company to a high degree of discipline, he had a number of good and reliable officers, and he had an experienced surgeon to watch over their health.

Besides, they were homeward bound.

But then so was the *Bounty* when the mutiny occurred.

[1] In westerly gales Matavai Bay is an unsafe anchorage. In 1788 the *Bounty* had a narrow escape from being blown ashore and in 1802 the *Norfolk* was driven ashore and became a total wreck.

Like all naval captains, particularly at this time, Captain Edwards was a lonely man, dependent entirely upon his own wits and courage. There were no governors, consuls or indeed any British officials within a thousand miles with whom he could consult, or from whom he could obtain aid and advice. The most severe critics of Bligh and Edwards were all armchair critics. Sir John Barrow was a distinguished civil servant, for forty years Second Secretary of the Admiralty. He should have known better, occupying such a position, than to have published anonymously a book traducing an officer in the service which he had the honour of administering.[1]

Judge Andrew McFarland announced his opinion that Captain Edwards 'was a still greater savage than Bligh,'[2] language hardly becoming a judge and in contrast to Surgeon Hamilton who wrote:

Orders were given that the prisoners should be victualled in every respect the same as the ship's company, both in meat, liquor and all the extra indulgencies with which we were so liberally supplied. Captain Edwards very humanely commiserated with their unhappy and inevitable length of confinement.

Mutiny was in the air and the isolated case of the *Bounty*, with its special circumstances, was soon to be followed by serious and prolonged outbreaks in the British fleets.

Edwards had been brought up in a harsh coarse school, perhaps the hardest and most callous of all, a seafaring life in the eighteenth century, when 'I'm all right, Jack!' sounded the tone.

It was a period when Macaulay's description of the Carolean Navy was still partly true: 'Those who were seamen were not gentlemen and the gentlemen were no seamen.'

It is true that a new school was emerging, actuated as much by sentiments of humanity and gentleness as it was by its fighting vigour. But this was before Nelson's Band of Brothers had come to the front and cast its spell over the navy. Edwards was nearly sixty years of age when the Battle of the Nile was fought, but he was a boy of sixteen when Admiral Byng was executed for his failure to raise the siege of Minorca. The great crime was mutiny and the great sin was failure to fight, or to fight hard enough. Government and people wished to hear only of victories. It is possible that Admiral Jellicoe would have been executed had the Battle of Jutland been fought in the eighteenth century. Bligh and Edwards lived in times when the triangle and the gallows were there for all to see.

---

[1] *The Eventful History of the Mutiny of the 'Bounty'*.
[2] McFarland, *Mutiny in the 'Bounty'*.

Nor was it sufficient merely to abstain from mutiny or mutinous acts. No one could plead neutrality, and passivity was regarded as being tantamount to aiding and abetting.

If he reflected upon these circumstances at all, Captain Edwards must at times have referred to the precise phrasing of his Sailing Orders, the operative words of which were short and sharp:

'Bring 'em back, alive!'

These fourteen piratical villains would be in his charge not for a week or a month or two months, but for six or more months, during the trying passage home. It would indeed be a nerve-racking, dangerous navigation which would engage his time and his energies.

And there was the ever-present fear of collusion between his crew and the Fourteen. Captain Bligh, as Edwards well knew, had been taken completely and totally by surprise.

Chapter 15

High Value of Nails

WHEN Captain Wallis and the officers of the *Dolphin* returned to Europe in 1768, their reports of Tahiti or 'King George Island' not only aroused the suspicions of the Spanish Court but the interest of European savants. All this was increased by the similar and even more enthusiastic accounts of Bougainville and the rapturous phrases of 'Monsieur de Commerson, docteur en médicin &c.', Bougainville's surgeon-botanist in the *Boudeuse*.

This aura of romantic interest surrounded the very name of Tahiti for many years, or rather its many names, official and fancy. Among them were Isle de Cythère, apparently in reference to the ancient Cytherea, scene of Botticelli's *Birth of Venus*; *Utopia* of Sir Thomas More; the Fortunate Isle; and even the austere Darwin wrote of it as 'an island which must for ever remain classical to the voyager in the South Sea'.

*   *   *

Captain Bligh always maintained that the mutiny in his ship was due to the desire of the crew to return to Tahiti and enjoy the delights of that island, and to resume the connections that had been formed with the women there.

To assign the cause of such a revolution we can only imagine from the huzzas of the Mutineers that they have promised themselves greater pleasure and advantages at Otaheite than they were likely to meet with in their Native Country.

To this land of guile they are certainly returned, a Land where they need not labour and where the allurements of dissipation are more than equal to anything that can be conceived.[1]

The allurements of dissipation were indeed powerful influences on all ships' crews visiting Tahiti. Its discoverer, Captain Samuel Wallis, had made another discovery, too, that the fatal charms of the women had seriously disorganized the discipline of his ship. Finding it necessary to make an example, he flogged the Corporal of Marines and read the Articles of War.

[1] Bligh's Report.

68

The same applied to ships that visited Tahiti between the arrival of Captain Wallis in the *Dolphin* in 1767 and the *Pandora* in 1791. During these twenty-four years no fewer than twenty European ships had visited the island including English, French and Spanish vessels, and during that period accounts of the allurements of dissipation flew on the white wings of ships to every part of the globe.

The gallant tars deprived of their pleasures during many long sea passages landed in this paradise to find to their gratified delight that the fair islanders were quite uninhibited by the conventional codes of Christendom.

There was, however, one embarrassing hindrance to the sailors' free enjoyment of the island women. It appeared that neither gold nor silver was in demand but that the common iron nail was the fee demanded. The nail at once became the chief standard of local currency, whether in the purchase of pigs, chickens and fruits, or the fee demanded for female favours. At first the market struck a simple rate, one nail for a brief encounter and two for a night of love. The effect was at once apparent in the ships where a nail famine set in, the sailors removing every nail they could lay their hands on, with the result that the supply of nails declined as the price of love increased.

Despite these hindrances, the crews of ship after ship which continued to arrive over the next twenty years pressed home their eager attentions upon the ever-willing females. The subtle fascinations of the Gallic matelots and the more intense fires of the Iberian seamen vied with the ponderous onslaughts of the British tars.

The demand for nails seriously impaired the condition of the ship itself, as the first vessel to arrive at Tahiti had soon found. Captain Wallis of the *Dolphin* stated:

From this time, our market was very ill supplied, the Indians refusing to sell provisions at the usual price and making signs for larger nails. It was now thought necessary to look more diligently about the ship. . . . and it was soon found that all the belaying cleats had been ripped off and there that was scarcely one of the hammock nails left.

All hands were now ordered up and I practised every artifice to discover the thieves but without success.

Captain Cook had the same problem, as did the officers of every ship visiting Tahiti.

The reason for this demand for iron nails was due to the fact that iron was unknown to the Tahitians and nails proved to be very convenient for working up their fish hooks. These they made out of pearl shell which was very difficult to manipulate.

The sailing master of the *Dolphin*, George Robertson, has this anecdote about nails:

After dinner we sent the traders and waterers ashore, but when I was ordering the liberty men into the boat, the Carpenter came and tould me every cleat in the ship was drawn and all the Nails carryed off. At the same time the Boatswain informed me that the most of the hammock nails was drawen and the men obliged to lie on the deck for want of hammock nails. I immediately stopt the liberty men, and called All Hands and let them know that no man in the ship should have liberty to go ashore untill they informed me who drawd the nails and cleats and let me know what use they made of them.

But no one would acknowledge anything about drawing nails but all said they knowed the use they were put to.

Then some of the Young Gentlemen tould me that all the Liberty men carried on a trade with the Young Girls who hade now rose their price for some days past, from a twenty or thirty penny nail, to a forty penny, and some was so Extravagant as to demand a Seven or Nine Inch Spick [spike], this was a plain proof of the way the large nails went.

This evening I observed a great murmuring among the crew (all leave having been stopped). I therefore stept forward to see if I could find out hou had drawen the nails and cleats. At this time the Galley was full, dressing their suppers and some blamed one, some another. It being dark, none of them observed me, therefore tould their mind plain. At last I found that the most of them was concerned and several said they had rather receive a dozen lashes nor have their Liberty stopt. At last there was a tryall amongst them, and six was condemned for spoiling the old trade by giving large Spick nails when others had only a hammock nail which was refused, they being much smaller than the Spicks, but two cleared themselves by proving that they got double value for the Spicks.[1]

The same George Robertson also relates an anecdote in which he was involved with 'the Queen'. This queen was the chieftainess Purea (named Oberea by Cook) and wife of the local chief, a woman of great strength of character and social influence. She now wished, it seems, to cultivate a more intimate relation with the *Dolphin*'s master.

The Queen took it in her head that I was painted (tatooed) after the manner of her country and therefore wanted to see my legs, thighs, and arms. Rather nor disoblige her, I showed her all, which greatly surprised her. She would not believe that I showed her my skinn until she feelt it with her own hands. She then wanted to see my breast which I likewise showed her, but it surprised her most of all my breast being full of hair.[2]

[1] Carrington (ed.), *The Discovery of Tahiti*.
[2] The bodies of the Tahitians were generally hairless.

Captain Peter Heywood RN, 1773–1831

Captain Bligh

George Hamilton,
Surgeon RN

She supposed I was a very strong man and began to feel my thighs and legs to know if they had the strength they seem to have. I then put my legs in position that they feelt both stiff and strong which made her look very hard in my face and calld out with Admiration Oh! Oh! Oh! and desired the Chief to feel my legs which I allowed him to do. They then hade a long talk and the Queen lade hould of me to lift me up, but I prevented her, without her being sensible of the reason why she could not lift me up. This surprized her most of all and she called Oh Oh. The Chief made a sign to me to lift her up, which I did with one arm and carried her round the Cabin. This seemed to please her greatly and she eyed me all round and to be very merry and cheerful. If I am not mistaken by her Majy's behaviour afterwards, this is the way the Ladys here trys the men, before they admit them to be their lovers.

The person of the king was sacred and inviolable, the royal issue being the fruit of the immortal gods, who were worshipped only in spirit, idolatry being unknown. But blood sacrifices were in full force, the victims always being males. The immense number of ceremonial blood sacrifices plus the ravages of war naturally led to a preponderance of females, but this was counteracted by the simple device of every other female child being put to death at birth. As the husband always officiated as accoucheur to his wife, the child was instantly destroyed as soon as the sex was seen.

Surgeon Hamilton refers to the practical communism that prevailed in Tahiti:

A native of this country divides everything in common with his friend. The extent of the word friend by them is bounded only by the universe. Was he reduced to his last morsel of bread he cheerfully halves it with him. Rank makes no distinction in hospitality, for king & beggar relieve each other in common. The English are allowed by the rest of the world to be a generous charitable people but the Ota-heitians could not help bestowing the most contemptuous word in their language upon us which is Peery Peery, or Stingy.

Nor did this devotion to his friend or Tyo (Tayo, Taio) exclude a similar devotion to his wife.

In becoming the Tyo or friend of a man, it is expected to pay him a compliment by cherishing his wife. Being ignorant of that ceremony, I very innocently gave high offence to Matuara, the king of York Islands[1] to whom I was introduced as his friend or Tyo. A shyness took place on the side of his Majesty from my neglect to his wife. Through the medium of Brown the interpreter[2] he put me in mind of my duty. On my promising my endeavours, matters were for that time made

---

[1] The neighbouring island of Moorea adjacent to Tahiti.
[2] John Brown from the *Mercury*.

up. It was to me however a very serious inauguration. I was, in the first place, not a young man, and had been on shore a whole week. The lady was a woman of rank, being sister to Ottoo, the king of Otaheiti and had in her youth been beautiful, and named Peggy Otoo. She is the right hand dancing figure so elegantly delineated in Cook's *Voyages*. But Peggy had seen much service and bore many honourable scars in the fields of Venus. However, his Majesty's service must be done, and Matuara and I were again friends. He was a domesticated man and passionately fond of his wife and children; but now he became pensive and melancholy, dreading the child should be Piebald, though the lady was six months advanced in her pregnancy before we came to the island.

The sailors chased the girls only to find the girls were not chaste. The social and moral code, as the sailors knew it, was here completely reversed. The females made the approaches to the males and exhibited their charms with a naïve innocence that enchanted the honest tars.

The accounts of the English, Spanish and French captains contributed to form and to confirm the sentimental conception of an innocent primitive society hitherto free from the world's slow stain. Here was the noble savage, pure and uncontaminated, so pure that far from sex being synonymous with sin, the conception of sin itself was unknown to them. Chastity far from being a state of grace was viewed as disgrace.

It was such a country, no doubt, before the coming of the white man, a Pacific paradise where ethical and moral standards were the very antithesis of Western Christendom, where life, liberty and the pursuit of happiness were the ideal, and where no man need labour since nature provided all.

Chapter 16

Paradise Lost

M. DE BOUGAINVILLE'S surgeon-botanist in the frigate *Boudeuse*, Dr Philibert de Commerson, was another European savant who was dazzled by his first view of this enchanting island and its people:

My opinion of this island was such that I had already given it the name of Happy Island or Utopia which Thomas Morus [Sir Thomas More] had used for his ideal Republic: my name suited a land – perhaps the only one in the world – peopled by men without vice, without prejudice, without need, without dissension.

They are born under the loveliest of skies, fed by the fruits of a fertile soil which needs no cultivation, ruled by patriarchs rather than by kings. They know no other god but Love. To him every day is consecrated, the whole island is his temple, all the women are its idols and all the men its worshippers.

And what women they are! Rivals of the women of Georgia in beauty, unveiled sisters of the Graces! Shame and prudery have no tyranny here; the lightest of gauze coverings move at the command of every breeze and every desire. The act of procreation is an act of worship; its prelude is encouraged by the prayers and song of the whole assembled people and its consummation is hailed by general applause. All strangers are allowed to share in these happy mysteries; it is even one of the duties of hospitality to invite them; thus the good Tahitian always enjoys either the sensation of his own pleasures or the sight of those of others. Some severe censor perhaps will only see in this a total collapse of moral sense, loathsome prostitution and a most shameless cynicism; but is this not the state of Natural Man, born essentially good, free of all preconceived ideas, who follows, without defiance and without shame, the pleasant impulses of an instinct that is always sure, because his reason has not yet become degenerate?[1]

In his poem 'The Island' Byron rhapsodized over the beauty of the South Sea isles:

> Before the winds blew Europe o'er these climes.
> True they had vices – such are Nature's growth –
> But only the barbarians – we have both;

Corney, *Quest and Occupation of Tahiti.*

73

The sordor of civilization, mix'd with all the savage
Which Man's fall hath fixed.
Who such would see may from his lattice view
The Old World more degraded than the New.

Tahiti in particular he painted in gorgeous colours:

Nature, and Nature's goddess – woman – woos
To lands where, save their conscience, none accuse;
Where all partake the earth without dispute
And bread itself is gathered as a fruit.
Where none contests the woods, the fields, the streams –
The gold-less age, where gold disturbs no dreams,
Inhabits or inhabited the shore
Till Europe taught them better than before:
Bestow'd her customs and amended theirs
But left her vices also to their heirs.

The English sailor in the *Dolphin* who sold information about Tahiti to the Spanish ambassador (vide page 9) wrote in his account for the ambassador:

They soon became very tractable and brought gifts of food of every description, and even to offer their wives and daughters to the crew of the ship. The medium of exchange consisted of nails that they were very keen after, iron being entirely unknown and nails proving very convenient for working up their fish hooks that they make out of pearl shell which is very difficult to manipulate. In fact nails of different sizes became the price not only of the various commodities but also of the favours of the women of this island who were eager to yield themselves to members of the crew.

Midshipman Henry Ibbot of HMS *Dolphin* recorded in his Journal:

The men most wear their beards and most go naked except a bag where they put their privities. Some women are quite white and had a red colour in their faces. They are in general small but quite handsomely featured. One thing very remarkable which I never heard of any People before that is both Men and women having their backsides black'd, and some of the old men which is done by pricking it in (tatoo-ing).

Their love of Iron [nails] is so great that the women or rather Girls, for they were very young and small, prostitute themselves to any of our people for a Nail, hardly looking at Knives, Beads or any toy. Yet I must say the Girls which were of the white sort would admit of any Freedom, but the last, every one having by what I saw a Man or Husband.

The introduction of venereal disease into the island, whether by the English or French ships, was but a symptom of the general degeneration that followed the impact of Western civilization upon these 'innocents' of the Pacific. Perhaps the disease existed in a latent form among the natives of Polynesia long before the advent of Europeans, and possibly the latter are innocent of the charge.

At any rate, before the end of the eighteenth and during the early years of the nineteenth century, a shattering blow to the native culture, morale and ethic had been struck.

As early as 1792, soon after Edwards' departure from Tahiti, when Bligh returned there on his Second Voyage, he was struck by the change in the natives since his previous visit:

The quantity of old clothes left among these people is considerable. They wear such rags as truly disgust us. It is rare to see a person dressed in a neat piece of [native] cloth which formerly they had in abundance and wore with much elegance. Their general habiliments are now a dirty shirt and an old coat and waistcoat. They are no longer clean Otaheitians but in appearance a set of ragamuffins with whom it is necessary to observe great caution.[1]

Matavai, that once beautiful Garden of Eden was, it seems, rapidly becoming a European slum.

But worse was to follow from the constantly growing tide of whalers, traders, missionaries, blackbirders and beachcombers who flocked there.

To these noble savages or poor creatures, however they were viewed, sex was as natural a function as breathing, in which there was no element of shame or selfconsciousness. It was conducted in public, and applauded in public.

But now came a totally new doctrine. Christianity in the persons of the missionaries arrived with the new teaching – sex was sin, a conception which these poor lost creatures were quite unable to understand or to assimilate. Tahitian maidens, maidens or no, hitherto nude from the waist up and nearly nude below, must conceal their erogenous zones beneath Christian clothing, repress their natural desires, repel Tahitian youth, and teach these wayward gallants the new gospel, sex=sin.

Gradually the early European notions of this island paradise became modified and finally died in the light of present-day reality, but the tradition and the appeal still lingered, drawing such artists as Gauguin to

[1] Bligh also noted: 'Our friends here have benefited little from their intercourse with Europeans. Our men have taught them such vile expressions as are in the mouth of every Otaheitian, and I declare that I would rather forfeit anything than to have been in the list of ships that have touched here.'

'a riot of light and vegetation among a gentle people', and romanticists such as Pierre Loti to whom it was a spiritual home.

According to Captain F. W. Beechey in his *Narrative of a Voyage to the Pacific*, there had taken place a serious deterioration in the islanders by the time he visited them in 1830. This was more than sixty years after the first discovery of Tahiti by Captain Wallis:

All their usual and innocent amusements have been denied by the missionaries and these poor people, in lieu of them, have been driven to seek for resources in habits of indolence and apathy. That simplicity of character which atoned for many of their faults has been converted into cunning and hypocrisy. Poverty, drunkenness and disease have thinned the population to a frightful degree. A survey by the first missionaries in 1797 estimated the population at 16,000 souls. Captain Waldegrave in 1830, on the authority of a census, stated the population to be only 5,000, and there is too much reason to ascribe this diminution to praying, psalm singing and dram drinking.

The Europeans came bringing the message of the Gospel and the benefits of Christendom and of Western civilization, but there were those who thought that the last state of the Tahitians was worse than the first.

Surgeon Hamilton seems to have been among them:

Happy would it have been for those people had they never been visited by Europeans; for to our shame be it spoken, disease and gunpowder is all the benefit they have ever received from us, in return for their hospitality and kindness. The ravages of the venereal disease is evident, from the mutilated objects so frequent amongst them, where death has not thrown a charitable veil over their misery, by putting a period to their existence.

Wallis, Bougainville and Cook were all three anxious to avoid introducing venereal disease into the island, and took every possible precaution to avoid such a disaster.

The surgeon of the *Dolphin* 'affirmed upon his Honour' that no man on board was affected with any sort of disorder that they could communicate to the natives of this beautiful island.

Bougainville stayed at Tahiti for ten days only. Captain Cook when at Tahiti during his Second Voyage, wrote:

Apa no Pretane[1] (English disease) though they, to a man say it was brought to the isle by M. de Bougainville, but they thought M. Bougainville came from Pretane as well as every other ship that has touched at the isle. Were it not for this assertion of the natives, and none of Captain Wallis' people being affected with the venereal

[1] Pretane = Britain.

disease, either while at Otaheite, or after they left it, I should have concluded that long before these islanders were visited by Europeans this or some disease akin to it had existed among them.

When Cook arrived at Tahiti on his First Voyage, two years after the *Dolphin* and one year after the *Boudeuse*, venereal disease developed immediately, within a fortnight. When he sailed, after a stay of three months, twenty-four of the fifty sailors and nine of the eleven Marines were under treatment, though all had been reported to be clear of disease by the surgeon at the time the *Endeavour Bark* passed Cape Horn on the outward passage.

And yet, within a fortnight of their arrival in Matavai Bay, cases were being treated by the surgeon and it spread rapidly. This seems to prove conclusively that Cook's men were not at fault.

As for the visits of the Spanish ship, these came three and five years after Cook's *Endeavour*. But the disease seems to have been well established by the time of Captain Edwards' arrival in the *Pandora*.

After the ship had sailed from Tahiti, Surgeon Hamilton recorded: 'We now began to discover that the ladies of Otaheite had left us many warm tokens of their affection.'

Chapter 17

The Schooner Disappears

WHEN he finally sailed from Matavai Bay on 8 May 1791, with the schooner *Resolution* in company, Captain Edwards had completed only a part of his mission. Where were the Nine, including Christian the chief mutineer, and the *Bounty*? In search of them, Edwards now set out on a prolonged cruise among the islands, visiting in turn a very large number. Among those he visited, still with the schooner in company, were Huaheine, Ulitea, Otaha, Bolobola and others of the Society group adjacent to Tahiti.

Then he steered west to the Cook Islands for Aitutaki, sending the boat on shore, first covered by the schooner against a surprise attack. A similar visit was made to Palmerston Island, where cutter, launch and jolly boat were sent on shore, the date being 22 May 1791.

Lieut. Corner returned with the news that they had found a yard marked '*Bounty*'s Driver Yard' *and other circumstances* that indicated that the *Bounty* was, or had been there. As Palmerston Island consists of nine small islands joined by a tree-covered reef, these various islets occupied a long time in the search by the schooner and the *Pandora*'s boats, all of which were well-armed against a surprise attack by the *Bounty* people.

The truth was that the flotsam and jetsam indicated not that the *Bounty* had visited Palmerston Island, but that she had not visited it. While at Tubuai, Christian had either landed or lost some spare spars and rigging when the *Bounty* was warped closer inshore. (See page 20.)

This flotsam had been caught up in the south-east trade wind and surface current and had drifted, in twenty-three months, from Tubuai to Palmerston, a distance of 900 miles, passing a dozen islands and reefs on the way. After reflection, Edwards himself came to this conclusion:

The driver yard was probably drove from Tubuai where the *Bounty* lost the greater part of her spars and as no recent traces could be found on the island of a human being or any part of the wreck of a ship, I gave up all further search and hopes of finding the *Bounty* or her people there.

He therefore recalled the schooner and boats, but the jolly boat did not return. This smallest of the *Pandora*'s boats was in charge of Midshipman John Sivall, RN, who had a crew of four men, including a son of *Pandora*'s bo'sun. Both ship and schooner made a protracted search for her but nothing was found and the crew's fate remained unknown.

Captain Edwards wrote:

The ship and the tender cruized about in search of the boat until 29 May (i.e. for five days) seeing nothing of her. I being well in with the land, sent on shore once more to examine the reef and beach of the northernmost island but with no success. Neither the boat nor any article belonging to her could be found.

Hamilton wrote:

It may be difficult to surmise what has been the fate of these unfortunate men. They had a piece of salt beef thrown into their boat on leaving the ship and it rained a good deal that night and the following day which might satiate their thirst.

Anything may have happened to the boat's crew. They may have been massacred by the islanders; they may have been drowned in the fierce surf which runs very high at Palmerston making landing dangerous and in many places impracticable. Corner and Hayward both wore cork jackets when landing but even so had they not been expert swimmers would have drowned.

The fresh south-east wind which was blowing might have swept the boat out to sea, to the north-west. The nearest land in that direction is the Samoans, but these islands lie 600 miles away and the boat's crew could have died of starvation and thirst. Nor would Midshipman Sival have had any idea of his whereabouts but only a general idea of direction from his boat's compass. Even this would be of little help, since his boat would be more or less at the mercy of the prevailing wind.

Captain Edwards was placed in a harsh dilemma and cannot be charged with callousness in eventually sailing away. According to his own official report, confirmed by Surgeon Hamilton, his search was prolonged and methodical and extended over a period of five days during which masthead look-outs, the schooner and the ship's cutter were all engaged in the search, not to mention the anxious watch of every man on board.

Surgeon Hamilton adds a note on the islanders

who are tempted to dare the elements and from their temerity are often blown to remote and uninhabited islands. Distressing incidents of this nature often happening to inhabitants of the South Seas, they now seldom undertake any hazardous enterprise by water without a woman and a sow with pig being in the canoe with them; by which means if they are cast on an uninhabited island, they fix their abode.

Edwards now sailed to the north-west, bound for the Duke of York's island which was reached on 6 June. The schooner and two boats were sent on shore to examine the island which the discoverer Commodore Byron had reported to be uninhabited. Edwards writes:

As Mr. Byron described the island to be without inhabitants the sight of some houses and the finding of a ship's large wooden buoy of foreign make, before they were minutely examined wrot so strongly on the minds of our people that they saw many things in imagination that did not exist. All tended to persuade them that the *Bounty*'s people were really upon the island agreeable to the intelligence given by Hillbrant.[1]

After a prolonged search, Edwards sailed on to discover New Land, the island of Nukunono, another of the Union group and well populated. Strenuous efforts were made to get into touch with these islanders as it was thought they might be able to give news of the *Bounty*, but they were shy and nervous and disappeared when approached, and Edwards gave up the search after laying down the position of the new island on the chart.

The *Pandora* was well equipped for survey and chart work, having on board a reliable chronometer and two skilled navigators in the ship's master, Mr Passmore, and the navigating lieutenant, Mr Hayward. Nevertheless, the problem of finding accurate longitudes remained. Edwards wrote:

There is so great a difference in the situation of this island [Duke of York's] as laid down in the charts of Hawkesworth and of Captain Cook that there may be some doubt as to its real situation. I followed that of Captain Cook yet our account did not exactly agree with him. He lays it down in Long. 173° 3′ West yet our account by observation is 172° 6′ and by timekeeper 172° 39′.

[1] Hillbrant, one of the mutineers, had told Edwards that Fletcher Christian had told him the evening before he sailed from Tahiti 'destination unknown' that he intended to sail to an uninhabited island discovered by Commodore Byron in 1765 and named by him Duke of York's island but now known as Oatafu, of the Union group. Christian might have 'planted' this idea in Hillbrant's mind to confuse and mislead a future search for him. The real fact was of course that Christian had sailed up-wind, against the Trade Wind while Edwards had gone down-wind, with the Trade.

In other words, a difference of twenty-four miles by chronometer and fifty-seven miles by observation. The discovery of Nukunono was quite accurately charted by Edwards as being in longitude 171° 31′ W. compared with its modern position of 171° 38′ W., a difference of seven miles only.

Continuing his search for the *Bounty* – a quite fruitless search since she no longer existed, and Christian and his men were at the other side of the vast Pacific Ocean – Edwards ran due south to the Samoa group which both ship and tender explored for several days. Here a fresh disaster befell.

On the evening of 22 June while ship and tender were off Upolu, the tender was lost to sight during a tropical rain squall. Flares were burned and guns fired and Edwards cruised around for two days searching for the little *Resolution* without result. He was greatly concerned, because the islands were occupied by hostile people always ready to attack and the little schooner with only a master's mate in command, a midshipman, a quartermaster and six Marine privates might have been overwhelmed by an attack in force, or by guile.

Another cause for disquiet was that she was short of food and water. These were actually ready on deck to give her in the morning and according to Surgeon Hamilton she had on board only 'a small cag of salt and another of nails and iron ware to traffic with the Indians'.

However the master's mate, Mr Oliver, had been told by Edwards that if he did get separated from the *Pandora* he was to make for the rendezvous at Anamooka. Among the safeguards for the schooner's crew against being boarded and slaughtered by armed natives was a boarding netting all round the bulwarks. Furthermore, it was, in the circumstances, fairly well armed against ignorant natives, having several blunderbusses and barrelled pieces on board, which were most effective in keeping at bay natives who had no experience of gunpowder.

For two days after they were separated, *Pandora* cruised around the south-east of Upolu looking for the schooner.

In the morning the schooner was not to be seen. We cruised about for her in sight of the island (Upolu) on the 23rd and the 24th and as I could not find her near the place where she was first lost, I thought it better to make the best of my way to Anamooka, the place appointed as a last rendezvous, and to endeavour to get there before her, lest her small force should be a temptation to the natives to attack her. We accordingly stood to the southward and on 29th anchored in Anamooka Road.[1]

[1] Edwards' Report.

On the way they encountered heavy tropical rains which drenched everybody on board and incommoded the prisoners in the box who complained that 'Pandora's Box' was leaky. They applied to the first lieutenant, John Larkan, who replied: 'Well, I'm wet, too, and everybody on deck, and it will dry when the weather clears up.'

According to Morrison's *Journal*, Larkan was more severe on the prisoners than Captain Edwards, who to his dismay on arriving at Anamooka found no sign of the schooner of which he had lost sight on 22 June.

Whilst we were watering the ship &c I sent Lieut. Hayward to the Happys (Happai) Islands in a double canoe which I hired of Tooboo, a chief of these islands, for the purpose of examining them and to make enquiries after the *Bounty* and the tender, but no intelligence could be got of either of these vessels at these two islands, nor at either of the Happy Islands, and having completed our water and got a plentiful supply of yams and a few hogs, we sailed (from Anamooka) on 10th July.

Surgeon Hamilton wrote:

Immediately on our arrival at Anamooka a large sailing canoe was hired and Lieut. Hayward and one Marine private sent to the Happy Islands to make enquiry after the *Bounty* and our tender, but received no intelligence.

Whatever this trip in the canoe by Hayward implied, it is not clear where the so-called Happy Islands were to which he went. As a glance at the map will show, the whole group has, at one time or another, been named the Haa'pai Group, or the Friendly Islands or the Tongatabu Group, their present designation, numbering in all some 150 islands of which thirty-six are inhabited.

During the ten days he lay at Anamooka, Edwards had been in close contact with the chief and high priest of the island groups. His name was Fatafehi and says Edwards, 'he was generally acknowledged to be the superior chief of all the islands known under the names of the Friendly, Happy, and also of many other islands unknown to us'.

Edwards was anxious to enlist the friendship and confidence of this influential chieftain who seems, however, to have been rather deceitful and a bit of a liar. Edwards embarked Fatafehi in the *Pandora* when she sailed on 10 July for a cruise of the islands, beginning with Tofoa, forty-five miles away. Edwards was very much aware of the need for maintaining friendly relations with such an influential figure as Fatafehi. He knew only too well of the savage attack by the Tofoans on Bligh's boat party fifteen months before, and he was increasingly concerned for the safety of the schooner.

I knew that Fatafehi wished to make a tour of the islands and invited him to come with us to Tofoa and Kao, two islands I intended to visit, as I thought he would be useful by procuring us a favourable landing at Tofoa, the island whose inhabitants had behaved so treacherously to Lt. Bligh when he put in there for refreshments in the *Bounty's* launch.[1]

Fatafehi the king was going to collect tribute from the islands under his jurisdiction and went in the *Pandora* to Tofoa; but before sailing, a letter was left to Mr. Oliver, the commander of the schooner should he chance to arrive before our return, with Macacala, a principal chief at Anamooka. On our way in the night the burning mountain on Tofoa exhibited a very grand spectacle; and in the morning when we arrived off Tofoa two canoes were sent on shore to announce the arrival of those two great personages Fatafehi and Toobou.

They went on shore at Tofoa in the *Pandora's* barge to give them more consequence; but the tributary princes of Tofoa came off in canoes to do homage to Fatafehi before he reached the shore. They came alongside the barge, lowered their heads over the side of the canoe and Fatafehi agreeable to their custom put his foot upon their heads. When on shore, what present he had received from us, he distributed among his subjects with a liberality worthy of a great prince.

Lieut. Corner went on shore with them to search and to make enquiries after the *Bounty* and our tender and then crossed over to Kao to do the same. At four in the afternoon Lt. Corner, Fatafehi and Toobou returned on board without success in their search and enquiries. We put them on board their canoes and they set out for Anamooka.

I now intended to visit Tongatabu but as the wind was southerly and unfavourable for the purpose, I decided to visit Oattooah (Upolu) once more in search of the *Bounty* and the schooner.[2]

This was on the evening of 11 July when the *Pandora* sailed away from Tofoa and Kao, steering north for Upolu.

MOVEMENTS OF PANDORA AND SCHOONER

1791

22 June	..	*Pandora* and schooner lose sight of each other off Upolu
23 June	..	*Pandora* looking for schooner
		Schooner looking for *Pandora*
24 June	..	*Pandora* sails south for Anamooka rendezvous
		Schooner sails south for Anamooka rendezvous
29 June	..	*Pandora* arrives at Anamooka rendezvous
		Schooner arrives at Tofoa

[1] Edwards' Report.   [2] Ibid.

30 June	..	Schooner leaves Tofoa and sails west, into the blue
10 July	..	*Pandora* leaves Anamooka
11 July	..	*Pandora* passes Tofoa
16 July	..	*Pandora* arrives Upolu in search of schooner.

Edwards arrived at Upolu on 16 July. Here he made further enquiries about the schooner, for it was hereabouts that she had been last seen and it seemed fairly obvious that the natives would have seen her. But though he had frequent communications with them and pressed his enquiries, the natives were not able or did not choose to know anything about the schooner. This was not surprising seeing that they had made a determined attack upon her less than a month before, i.e. on the night of 22 June, the very night on which she had disappeared from *Pandora's* view.

At length, after eighteen days' ineffectual search, Edwards returned to Anamooka on 28 July, the arranged rendezvous, expecting or at least hoping to find the schooner there. Instead, he experienced more trouble with the natives 'who robbed and stripped some of our people that were separated from the party'.

This was particularly annoying, for Edwards desired to be on the most friendly terms with these Friendly Islanders. He depended upon them to give aid and comfort to the schooner should she arrive there, and the *Pandora* herself required wooding, watering and provisioning.

One of the natives assaulted Lieut. Corner, who shot him dead. Edwards invited the principal chief on board to dine with him and when the chief learned that one of his people had been shot by Corner, he became very agitated. Edwards wrote:

I told him that the Lieutenant had been struck and that he and his party had been robbed of several things and that I was very glad the man had been shot and that I should shoot every person who attempted to rob us but that no other person except the thief should be hurt by us on that account. The axes and some other things that had been stolen were now returned and very few robbings of any consequence were attempted and discovered until the day of our departure.

By thus including an unimportant incident in some detail in his report to the Admiralty, Edwards was guarding himself against any complaints that he had needlessly become involved in hostilities with the natives.

The government at home were particular about this, recognizing that in the future if any colonies, trade or plantations were established, the establishment of friendly relations with the natives was essential and would give them an advantage over possible rivals such as Spain or France.

Edwards also 'took this opportunity of showing the chief what execution the cannon and carronades would do, by firing a six-pound shot on shore, and an eighteen-pounder loaded with grape into the sea'.

Thereafter the wooding and watering parties carried on their business without interruption, and Edwards showed his appreciation by going on shore himself and handing out gifts to the chief and others.

Chapter 18

Among the Islands

IT was now 2 August and Edwards had been engaged in his search for the *Bounty* since leaving Tahiti on 8 May, eighty-six days previously. He had been unable to find the schooner and he had had an anxious time with the natives at Anamooka. Surgeon Hamilton had something to say about these islanders:

The people of Anamooka are the most daring set of robbers in the South Seas. With the greatest deference and submission to Captain Cook, I think the name of Friendly Isles is a perfect misnomer, as their behaviour to himself, to us and to Captain Bligh's unfortunate boat at Murderers' Cove pretty clearly evinces. Indeed, Murderers' Cove in the Friendly Isles is saying a volume on the subject. . . .

The women here are extremely beautiful and although they want that feminine softness of manners which the Tahiti women possess in so eminent a degree, their matchless vivacity and fine animated countenances compensate the want of the softer blandishments of their sister isle. . . .

Many beautiful girls were brought on board for sale by their mothers who were very exorbitant in their demands, as nothing less than a broad axe would satisfy them; but after standing their market three days, *la pucelage* fell to an old razor, a pair of scissors, or a very large nail. Indeed this trade was pushed to so great a height that the quarterdeck became the scene of the most indelicate familiarities. Nor did the unfeeling mothers commiserate with the pain and suffering of the poor girls but seemed to enjoy it as a monstrous good thing. It is customary here, when girls meet with an accident of this kind, that a council of matrons is held and the noviciate has a gash made in her forefinger. We soon observed a number of cut fingers among them, and had the razors held out, I believe all the girls in the island would have undergone the same operation.

Sir Basil Thomson comments:

Had Captain Edwards known that Fatafehi (high priest and chief) who so loudly condemned the treachery to Bligh's boat party and had assured Edwards that nothing had been seen of the schooner, although he had heard of the abortive attack upon her, then Edwards would have taught them a lesson that would have lasted many years.

O–Tu–Nui, Lord Paramount
of Tahiti (Otoo)

The Island of Otahaite

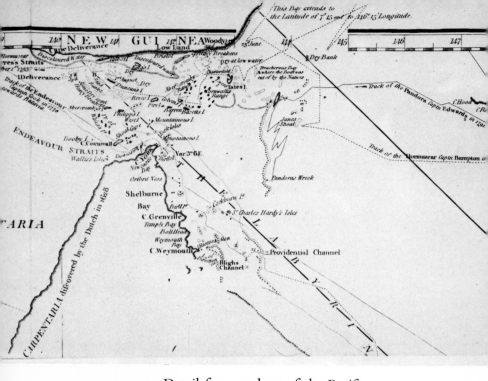

Detail from a chart of the Pacific
published by Laurie & Whittle, *c.* 1798

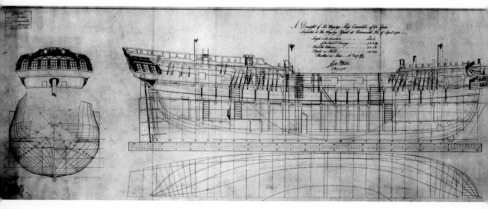

Draught of a frigate of *Pandora*'s class

For these 'Norsemen of the Pacific' whom Captain Cook, knowing nothing of the treachery they had planned against him under the guise of hospitality, had mis-named the Friendly Islanders were, in reality, a nation of wreckers.

For all practical purposes, Edwards had exhausted the possibilities of his 'police mission'. He had made a prolonged search of many islands since leaving Matavai Bay on 8 May, but in the wrong region of the Pacific. He had missed the *Bounty* by a narrow margin when in the neighbourhood of Pitcairn on his outward passage to Tahiti, without knowing it. He had lost a boat's crew at Palmerston Island, and the schooner and her crew at Upolu. Nine months had passed since he had left England. Every day and every night had brought unknown and unseen dangers. All the waters were uncharted; fearful hurricanes occasionally swept the islands. He had more than 170 souls on board including the mutineers; a long and hazardous passage back to England confronted him, and he had met with only partial success in apprehending the least guilty of the mutineers.

He had discovered and charted with considerable accuracy a large number of islands, islets, coral reefs, shoals and other navigational hazards and despite harassment from natives, he had maintained friendly relations generally.

All in all, he can hardly be said to have failed in his mission and the loss of the boat and the schooner were in no wise due to any shortcoming on his part. He wrote in his Report to the Admiralty:

On the 2nd August, 1791, having completed my water &c. and thinking it time to return to England, I did not think proper to wait any longer for the tender, but left instructions for her commander should she happen to arrive after my departure. I sailed from Anamooka, attended by a number of chiefs and canoes belonging to those and the surrounding islands. After the ship was under way, some of the natives had the address to get in at the cabin windows and stole from the cabin some books and other things, and they had actually got into their canoes before they were discovered. The thieves were allowed to make their escape, but the canoes that had stolen these things were brought alongside and broke up for firewood. During this transaction the other natives carried on their traffic alongside with as much unconcern as if nothing had happened.

So concluded the stay of HMS *Pandora* in and among the peoples of the Friendly or Tonga group of islands.

Today, after a century and a half of British protection and tutelage, this group with its happy, contented people fully justifies the appellation of Friendly Isles bestowed upon it at that time in error by Captain Cook, who was ignorant of the islanders' treacherous plots and plans to murder him and capture his ships.

In those days, few of the islanders had seen a European ship and were entirely ignorant of the nature of firearms. From a European standpoint, their morals were deplorable, the islands were torn by civil wars between rival chiefs, and the term 'savage barbarians' could justly be applied to them. All this was changed by the able warrior and administrator, the chief Toobou from whom Edwards had hired a double canoe. He succeeded after a long struggle in subduing all rival chiefs over the whole archipelago and was converted to Christianity by the first missionaries, he and his wife taking the names of George and Salote (Charlotte) in honour of George III and his consort.

These names have persisted in the Toobou dynasty to this day, the reigning sovereign Queen Salote being a prominent figure at the coronation of Queen Elizabeth II, having succeeded her father King George Toobou II in 1918. She is the direct descendant of Captain Edwards' Toobou.

Today, instead of the island of savage barbarians encountered by the *Pandora* and the little schooner *Resolution*, Tonga has a Parliament and a Speaker complete with mace. Instead of a visit from the solitary frigate of 1791, Tonga's annual shipping now totals 130,000 tons.

*   *   *

On 2 August 1791, Captain Edwards set sail from the Tonga islands on his return passage to England. He had been directed by the Admiralty to return via Endeavour Strait, which separates Australia from New Guinea, and thence via the Cape.

Before sailing, he made farewell presents to all the chiefs, and 'to many others of different descriptions' despite the fact they had made themselves a confounded nuisance by pilfering everything they could. Then the *Pandora* set forth, homeward bound.

Edwards steered due north along the meridian of 175° W. and passed within hailing distance of Tofoa whence Oliver in the schooner had fled thirty-four days earlier. Two days later, an island was sighted which Edwards supposed to be a new discovery and named Proby's Island. In fact, this island was Niua-fo'ou or New Niua which had first been seen by Captain Willem Cornelisz Schouten in his wonderful trading voyage round the world in 1615–17, 175 years before Edwards. He named it Good Hope island, but when he sent a boat on shore for water, the natives attacked it and Schouten was obliged to fire a volley that killed two of them. Since then, no other ship is known to have visited the island until the *Pandora* arrived. No doubt the memory of Schouten's visit had long since been forgotten, for when Edwards closed the island, they seemed to be friendly. As he said in his Report, 'The natives brought on board cocoanuts and plantains all of which I bought and made them a present of a few articles of iron. They told us they had water, hogs, fowls and yams on shore and plenty of wood. They spoke the same language as the Friendly Islands.'

Niua-fo'ou is today part of the territory of Queen Salote, and is reputed to grow the world's largest coco-nuts, and to be the home of the *Megapodius* or scrub hens, the eggs of which are prized as a delicacy by the Tongans. They are one of the family of mound birds so called on account of their throwing up large mounds of vegetable matter in which they deposit their eggs which they cover up and leave to be incubated by the heat produced by fermentation.

Still steering due north, Edwards now made for Uea Island discovered by Wallis a quarter of a century before in 1767. He says in his Report:

Canoes came off to us and brought us cocoanuts and fish which they sold for nails. I made them a present of some small articles which I always made a rule to do to first adventurers, hoping it might turn out advantageous to future visitors. They spoke the language of the Friendly Islands and I observed that one of the men had both his little fingers cut off.[1]

On leaving Uea Island Edwards turned almost a right-angle in his course and headed west by north, following in the track of his predecessors, Captain Carteret and Lieut. Bligh.

On 9 August, a week since he had left Anamooka, Edwards saw an island which he supposed to be a new discovery and named Grenville Island after the then Secretary of State for Foreign Affairs. It was in fact Rotumah Island.[2]

A great number of paddling canoes came off and viewed the ship at a distance and I believe their intentions were hostile. They were all armed with clubs and a great quantity of stones and joined in a kind of war whoop. We made signs of peace and offered them a variety of toys which drew them alongside, and then into the ship where they behaved very quietly. However they have the

---

[1] Mourning for the death of a chief or relation.
[2] Captain Edwards discovered and accurately charted five hitherto unknown islands, viz. Rotuma, Cherry, Mitre, Nukunono and Carysfort.

same propensity to thieving as the other islands and gave us many, some of which ludicrous examples.

The next day, at eleven in the morning, there was some alarm on board when the leadsman suddenly sang out: 'By the mark, eleven!' There was no land in sight and the sea hereabout averages 2,000 fathoms. Immediately afterwards, 'no bottom' was announced by the leadsman and the alarm passed. The spot was charted and named Pandora's Reef and so appears on the charts today but with the annotation E.D. (existence doubtful).

At noon on 13 August, having sailed 150 miles due west from Mitre and Cherry Islands, which he had discovered and named the day before, Captain Edwards sighted more land which he named Pitt's Island. This was Vanikoro in the Santa Cruz group. Edwards wrote: 'Although we were sometimes within less than a mile of the reef, we saw neither house nor people, yet we saw smoke very plain, from which it may be presumed that the island was inhabited.'

This brief remark conceals a curious incident in the annals of the Pacific Ocean. Three years before *Pandora* passed the island, in 1798 the French vessels *Boussole* and *Astrolabe* under the command of Le Comte de la Perouse were wrecked on the Vanikoro reefs, but their fate was not known to the outside world. In 1827, Captain Peter Dillon found a French sword hilt on Tikopia, an island 120 miles east-south-east of Vanikoro. On his return to England, he persuaded the East India Company to give him a ship so that he could make a thorough search for the French vessels. At Vanikoro he found the remains of the *Boussole*. The natives told him the *Astrolabe* had sunk in deep water. Dillon also found the clearing where the French survivors had felled timber to build the brig in which they had sailed away. Two of the crew had remained on Vanikoro, but one had died shortly before Dillon arrived, and one had left Vanikoro with some natives to go to another island. The relics which Dillon brought back are in the Louvre.

A few days later, 17 August, there was another alarm not in broad daylight but at midnight, when the lookout, a vigilant seaman named Wells, shouted 'breakers ahead!'

There was just time to wear ship, that is, to let her run off before the wind away from the breakers, and when day dawned they found themselves embayed in a dangerous reef, from which they had a providential escape.

The *Pandora* was now leaving behind the wide-open regions of the ocean and approaching the more narrow confines of the gulf formed by New Guinea and the Cape York Peninsula. As he approached the land, which lay both to north and south, Edwards was confronted by the difficulties and dangers of the Great Barrier Reef and the Torres Strait, 'the huge chaos of which remained unexplored'.

Chapter 19

The Wreck

THE odds against a ship passing safely through Torres Strait at this time were great. Torres had passed through in 1616. Cook won his way through only after prodigious and continual hazards, following a route which bore the unseen notice: Dangerous! Bligh had passed safely through in the *Bounty*'s launch, but the *Bounty*'s launch drew less than twenty-four inches. Now came the *Pandora* drawing fifteen to sixteen feet. Torres Strait is eighty to ninety miles in width and there are several possible passages, possible but not free from danger. Nowadays, with steamships which are under perfect control, which proceed quite independently of any wind that may be blowing, and which have all the modern charts and the help of lights and buoys, the risks are greatly diminished.

Edwards was alone. Unlike Bligh, who followed him a year later on his Second Voyage for the bread-fruit with two vessels *Providence* and *Assistant*, he was not able, as Bligh was, to send the *Assistant* ahead to sound out the way. What faced Edwards were a hundred coral reefs, breakers ahead and all round, head winds and the risk of being caught after dark without an anchorage, without any idea of what lay ahead, and with not a single warning beacon or light. Captain Cook wrote of his experiences:

Such are the vicissitudes attending this kind of service and must always attend an unknown navigation, was it not for the pleasure which naturally results to a man from being the first discoverer; even was it nothing more than sand and shoals, this service would be insupportable, especially in far distant parts like this, short of provisions and almost every other necessary.

The world will hardly admit of an excuse for a man leaving a coast unexplored he has once discovered. If dangers are his excuse, he is then charged with timorousness and want of perseverance, and pronounced the unfittest man in the world to be employed as a discoverer.

If, on the other hand, he boldly encounters all the dangers and obstacles he meets, and is unfortunate enough not to succeed, he is then charged with temerity and want of conduct.

There are three or four possible channels through Torres Strait from the east. The northernmost is Bligh Channel which Bligh traversed with difficulty in the following year. Edwards of course had no knowledge of it and was precluded from looking for it, as it was blocked by reefs and sandbanks.

The middle passage is that passed through by Flinders in the *Investigator* three years later. This passage had the advantage of giving an anchorage under the lee of Murray Islands and of a daylight passage through the Prince of Wales channel. Edwards was the discoverer of the Murray Islands which he now sighted. He steered towards them:

I then steered W by N until half past five when a reef was seen extending from the island a considerable way to the N.W., the island bearing W.S.W. I immediately hauled upon the wind in order to pass to the southward of it, the passage to the northward being obstructed. I stood on and off and was still during the night. In the morning (26 August) bore away. But as we drew near to the island we also saw a reef extending to the southward from the south end of the island.

Thus blocked in his attempt to reach the Murray islands, Edwards was forced to the southwards.

I ran to the southwards along the reef with the intention and expectation of getting round it. The whole day (Aug. 26) was spent without succeeding in my purpose, and without seeing the end of the reef, or any break in it that gave the least hopes of a channel fit for a ship.

And the whole night of 26 August, the whole day of 27 August, and the whole night of 27–28 August were also spent in this manner. It must have been a most anxious period for Edwards. Without knowing it, he was on the outer side of the northern section of the Great Barrier Reef which runs for 1,250 miles along the east coast of Australia.

A century later, the small barque *Otago* was probably the last ship to pass through Torres Strait under sail. Her master was Joseph Conrad. He was bound from Port Jackson to Mauritius and had chosen, with his owner's approval to make the passage north-about, instead of south-about, via the Great Australian Bight and the Leeuwin.

What would the memory of my sea life have been for me if it had not included a passage through Torres Strait in its fullest extent . . . along the track of the early navigators?

It was not without a certain emotion that I put her head at daybreak for Bligh Entrance and packed on her every bit of canvas I could carry. Windswept, sun lit, empty waters were all around me, half veiled by a brilliant haze. The first thing that caught my eye was a black speck – the wreck of a small vessel. . . . Thirty-six hours afterwards, of which about nine were spent at anchor, as I approached the other end of the Strait, I sighted a gaunt grey wreck . . . and thus I passed out of Torres Strait before the dusk settled upon its waters.

The sea has been for me a hallowed ground, thanks to those books of travel and discovery which had peopled it for me with unforgettable shades of the masters in the calling which, in a humble way, was to be mine too. These were men great in their endeavour and in hard-won successes of militant geography; men who went forth, each according to his lights and with varied motives but each bearing in his breast a spark of the sacred fire.[1]

On 25 August, the *Pandora* was well into the Strait and among the reefs. All hands on deck were at the first degree of readiness. Two leadsmen were in the chains on port and starboard bows, continuously calling the depth as they sounded. An officer was at the masthead conning the ship, the captain stood by the helmsman, the anchors were ready and everybody on the alert.

In later years some armchair critics, with the aid of the modern Admiralty charts, studying the tracks through Torres Strait of succeeding navigators and armed with all the experience of a century's surveys, have pointed out what Edwards should have done. He should have hugged the New Guinea coast and crept through that way or he should have done what Flinders did three years later in the *Ivestigator* and closed the Murray Islands and anchored safely there for the night. But Bligh and Flinders followed Edwards, they did not precede him. They had *his* experience; he did not have theirs. The critics ignore another important consideration. Edwards had specific orders from the Admiralty in writing. 'You are to examine and survey Endeavour Strait. . . .' Not any other strait or channel. He was not to go poking around Torres Strait, looking for trouble. Torres Strait was not mentioned in his sailing orders. He was to 'examine and survey' Endeavour Strait, the strait through which Captain Cook had passed homeward bound in 1771.

Endeavour Strait is located on the extreme southern boundary of Torres Strait of which it can hardly be said even to form part.

Sir Basil Thomson wrote:

By hugging the coast of New Guinea, the *Pandora* would have won a clear passage through these wreck-strewn Straits of Torres, but the navigators of those days counted on clear water to Endeavour Straits and recked little of the dangers of the Great Barrier Reef. Bligh chanced upon a passage in 12° 34' S Lat. so aptly that he called it *Providential Channel*.[2]

[1] Conrad, Joseph. 'Geography and Some Explorers'. *National Geographic Magazine*, Washington, March 1924.
[2] Edwards. *Voyage of HMS* Pandora.

But by 'hugging the coast of New Guinea' Edwards would have been contravening his orders to examine and survey Endeavour Strait which lay ninety miles to the south. To examine and survey Endeavour Strait, he would have to hug not the New Guinea coast but the coast of Cape York Peninsula. Sir Basil refers to Bligh's Providential Channel through the Barrier Reef. But this was not Bligh's but Captain Cook's channel. The entrance through which Bligh ran his boat is known as Bligh's Boat Entrance and the Admiralty Sailing Directions note that it is 'too narrow to be good for sailing vessels'.

While Edwards and his officers anxiously scanned the long line of breakers on the reef on the morning of the 28 August, they thought they saw the long-expected break in the reef. Lieut. Corner was at once ordered to go off in the yawl and have a closer look. He went to the top masthead before leaving the ship to have a good look round. Then with an axe, fuel, provisions, water and a compass he set out in the boat while the ship was hove to. Surgeon Hamilton was an eager onlooker.

At five in the afternoon a signal was made from the boat, that a passage through the reef was discovered for the ship. But wishing to be well informed in so intricate a business and the day being far spent, we waited the boat coming on board and made a signal to expedite her [return].

Night closing fast upon us and considering our former misfortunes of losing the tender and the jolly boat, rendered it necessary both for the preservation of the boat and the success of the voyage to endeavour by every possible means to get hold of her. False fires were burnt, and muskets fired from the ship and answered by the boat reciprocally; and as the flashes from their muskets were distinctly seen by us, she was reasonably soon expected on board. We sounded and had no bottom with a hundred and ten fathom line, till past seven o'clock when we got ground in fifty fathom. The boat was now seen close under our stern. We were lying-to to prevent the ship fore-reaching.

Immediately on sounding this last time (and getting only fifty fathoms) the topsails were filled.

But before the topsails filled to draw her off, the *Pandora* struck on the reef. At that instant the boat was hoisted on board.

Part II

Chapter 20

Pandora's End

UNLIKE air crashes, shipwrecks are or were usually prolonged and agonizing. In an air disaster, death looms up suddenly and almost instantaneously; in a shipwreck the calamity is seen approaching, the event is usually long drawn out and the end frequently delayed for hours, even days or weeks.

A sense of danger was present in the *Pandora* long before she struck. All hands were alive to it. The long impenetrable reef was there before them, visible in close proximity, too close. Sir Basil Thomson complains that Captain Edwards 'adopted a most dangerous practice of running blindly on through the night whereas his predecessors lay to till daylight. Now, in the most dangerous sea in the world, Captain Edwards threw this obvious precaution to the wind'.

Captain Edwards had been sailing in broad daylight since dawn, that is, for thirteen hours, before his ship struck on the reef. The ship had been backing and filling for seven hours, everyone anxiously watching and waiting for the boat that had been sent in to examine the opening of the reef; all hands were at their stations. By the time the boat signalled a passage through the reef at five o'clock, it was too late to attempt the passage, and with the memory of the lost jolly boat and the lost schooner, there was anxiety to recover the boat. The leadsmen were sounding continuously. One hundred and ten fathoms, no bottom! Then suddenly: Fifty fathoms! Danger! Make sail!

Too late!

Unlike the steamship whose engine-room telegraph's clamant demand for 'full speed astern!' or 'full speed ahead!' is instantly met, Captain Edwards had to rely upon the slow and laborious process of making sail, trimming sail, waiting for the wind to fill the sails, waiting for the ship to gain steerage way. In the darkness and from a moving ship he had to keep his eyes on the reef, on the boat and on the ship and his ears open for the leadmen's cries. At this crisis, the ship was hardly under control. As usual, the crisis came after darkness had fallen, after everyone had been exposed to the glare of the tropic sun during the day, and all hands were tired and dispirited. Now they were confronted with a night of toil and fear.

The seaward side of the reef rose like a sheer wall from the ocean depths, a jagged coral wall. It was on to the top of this wall that the *Pandora* had drifted. She struck so heavily on the reef and the coral was so jagged and hard that it tore her planking; the long lazy swell from seaward, as it thundered on to the reef, bounced the ship up and down. Later, Captain Edwards wrote in his Report, 'we perceived that the ship had beat over the reef where we now had ten fathoms of water'.

Surgeon Hamilton later recorded the scene:

All hands were turned to the pumps and to bale at the different hatchways. Some of the prisoners were let out of irons and turned to the pumps. At this dreadful crisis, it blew very violently; and she beat so hard upon the rocks that we expected her every minute to go to pieces. It was an exceeding dark stormy night; and the gloomy horrors of death presented us all round, being everywhere encompassed with rocks, shoals and broken water. About ten, she beat over the reef and we let go the anchor in fifteen fathom water.

The guns were ordered to be thrown overboard; and what hands could be spared from the pumps were employed thrumbing a topsail to haul under her bottom, to endeavour to fother her. To add to our distress one of the chain pumps gave way, and she gained fast upon us. The scheme of the topsail was now laid aside, and every soul fell to bailing and pumping. All the boats, except one, were obliged to keep a long distance off on account of the broken water and the very high surf running near us. We baled between life and death, for had she gone down before daylight, every soul must have perished. She now took a heel and some of the guns they were endeavouring to throw overboard run down to leeward, which crushed one man to death; about the same time, a spare topmast came down from the booms and killed another man.

The people now became faint at the pumps and it was necessary to give them some refreshment. We had luckily between decks a cask of excellent strong ale which we brewed at Anamooka. This was tapped and served regularly to all hands which was much preferable to spirits as it gave them strength without intoxication. During this trying occasion the men behaved with the utmost intrepidity and obedience, not a man flinching from his post. We continually cheered them at the pumps with the delusive hopes of its being soon daylight.

About half an hour before daybreak, a council of war was held. As she was then settling fast down in the water, it was their unanimous opinion that nothing further could be done for the preservation of the ship; and it was their next care to save the lives of the crew. To effect which, spars, booms, hencoops and everything buoyant was cut loose that when she went down, they might chance to get hold of something. The prisoners were ordered to be let out of irons. The water was now coming faster in at the gun ports than the pumps could discharge, and to this minute the men never swerved from their duty. She now took a very heavy heel, so much that she lay quite down on one side.

As for the Fourteen in the Cage, three of them, Coleman, Norman and McIntosh, had been released and turned to manning the pumps. This left eleven in the Cage.

According to Morrison's Journal:

At daylight, the boats were hauled up and most of the officers being on top of the Box, we observed that they were armed and preparing to go into the boats by the stern ladders.

We begged that we might not be forgot when by Captn. Edwards's order Josh Hodges the armourer's mate was sent down to take the irons off Muspratt, Skinner and Byrn and send them up, but Skinner, being too eager to get out, got hauled up with his handcuffs on, and the other two following him close, the scuttle was shut and barred before Hodges could get to it . . . He knocked off my hand irons, and Stewarts. I begged the master-at-arms to leave the scuttle open when he answered: 'Never fear, my boys, we'll all go to Hell together.' The words were scarcely out of his mouth, when the ship took a sally and a general cry of 'There she goes' was heard. The master-at-arms and the centinels rolled overboard and at the same instant we saw through the stern ports Captain Edwards astern, swimming to the pinnace which was some distance astern. . . . Burkitt and Hillbrant were yet handcuffed and the ship under water as far as the main mast and it was now beginning to flow in upon us.

Now the Devine providence directed Wm. Moulter (boatsn's Mate) to the place. He was scrambling up on the box and hearing our cries, took out the bolt and threw it and the scuttle overboard. Such was his presence of mind, tho' he was forced to follow instantly himself. On this, we all got out except Hillbrant. It was as much as I could do to clear myself before she sank. . . .

Seeing one of the gangways come up, I swam to it and saw Muspratt on the other end, having brought him up with it, but falling on the heads of several others, it sent them to the bottom.

The top of our prison having floated, I saw Heywood, Burkitt and Coleman and the first lieutenant (John Larkan) . . .

After having been about an hour and a half in the water, I reached the blue yawl and was taken up with several others.

Peter Heywood corroborates Morrison at this point:

Captain Edwards sent the corporal and amourer down to let some of us out of irons, but only three were suffered to go up, Muspratt, Skinner and Byrne. The scuttle was then clapped on again, the armourer had only time to let two persons out of irons, the rest except three, letting themselves out. Two of these three went down with them on their hands, and the third was picked up.[1]

[1] Tagart. *Memoir of Captain Peter Heywood.*

In the event, Stewart, Sumner, Skinner and Hillbrant were drowned. Morrison, Heywood, Millward, Burkitt, Byrne, Ellison, Muspratt, Norman, McIntosh and Coleman survived.

So perished four more of the *Bounty* mutineers.[1] Now there were ten.

All four left widows and children at Tahiti. Perhaps their blood and genes still circulate faintly to this day among their descendants on Tahiti, islanders who have no memories and no knowledge of those far-off events, in contrast to Pitcairn Island where the legend, the memory, and the blood is still strong. Or on Norfolk Island where even more descendants of the mutineers and their Tahitian wives flourish than on Pitcairn. Here the curious tourist may see the great-great-grandchildren of Christian and his followers and hear the barbarous Anglo-Tahitian patois they speak.

Surgeon Hamilton of the *Pandora* closes the account of the shipwreck:

One of the officers now told the captain who was standing aft that the anchor at our bow was under water, that she was then going, and bidding him farewell, jumped over the quarter into the water. The captain followed his example and jumped after him. At that instant she took her last heel and while everyone was scrambling up to windward, she sunk in an instant. The crew had just time to leap overboard, accompanying it with a most dreadful yell.

The cries of the men drowning in the water was at first awful in the extreme; but as they sunk and became faint, it died away by degrees.

[1] No doubt the unhappy quartet lost with the *Pandora* would have died a more agonizing and a more shameful death a few months later, had they survived to return to England. Captain Bligh's evidence was strong and emphatic against Stewart. In a letter to his wife, he wrote: 'Besides this villain Christian, see young Heywood, one of the ringleaders and beside him see Stewart, joined with him . . . I was every day rendering them some service. It is incredible! These very young men I placed every confidence in, yet these great villains joined with the most able men in the ship, got possession of the arms, and took the *Bounty* from me.' Quoted by Dr G. Mackaness, *Life of Vice Admiral William Bligh*.

Chapter 21

The Boats

So much for the wreck of the *Pandora*. What of Captain Edwards' management of affairs during that dreadful night? As regards the first period, there was really not much he or any other captain could have done. From the moment she struck the reef in the darkness, with the conditions then prevailing, she was doomed. 'We perceived that the ship had beat over the reef' – and in beating over the reef she had torn her bottom to pieces. When she beat over the reef into shallower and calmer water, she was in no condition to remain afloat. It was of no avail to let go anchors, to dump her guns, or to try to fother her dreadfully mangled bottom.

There is an ancient sea adage: never go aground with an anchor at your bows. The *Pandora* struck on the reef with all her anchors on board, but the circumstances formed an exception to the old sea rule. All the anchors would have been of no avail in holding the *Pandora* off the reef simply because there was no anchorage, only ocean depths.

The sequence just before she struck was: No bottom! Fifty fathoms! Bump!

Captain Edwards' immediate reaction was to put his four boats into the water, 'with a view to carrying out an anchor'.

But it was now dark and launching four boats takes time. Carrying out an anchor takes much time, especially in an open seaway in the dark. While this desperate effort was being made, the ship began striking heavily on the reef. Within five minutes, there was four feet of water in the hold, still rising.

Later, after she had 'beat over the reef' and was floating in ten fathoms inside the reef, at anchor, they tried to fother her with a sail. This was the traditional method of reducing leaks by hauling a sail under the bottom, 'but the leaks increased in so great a degree that we apprehended she would sink before daylight'.

*   *   *

The second phase of the shipwreck came at dawn when the dire facts became apparent. Some critics have accused Edwards of losing his head, but he kept it sufficiently to assemble his officers, with the result that the following document was written and signed before, or directly after, the ship was abandoned.

Pandora 29 August 1791

It being the unanimous opinion of the 3 Lieuts. and the Master that nothing further could be done for the preservation of H.M.'s ship, it was concluded as next expedient to endeavour to save the lives of the crew.

To the truth whereof we this day put our hands.

GEO. HAMILTON, Surgeon
G. I. BENTHAM, Purser.

Another charge laid against Edwards by various writers is that he cruelly kept his prisoners manacled in the Cage to drown. Even when the ship was about to founder, he gave no orders for their release. Had it not been for the master-at-arms dropping the keys of the handcuffs through the scuttle of the Cage the moment before he himself jumped overboard, and for the heroic assistance of the bo'sun's mate, William Moulter, they would all have been drowned. As it was, Stewart, Hillbrant, Sumner and Skinner were drowned, two of them in manacles. This was atrocious behaviour on Edwards' part and cannot be condoned. There was absolutely no rhyme nor reason for it. It was, in modern parlance, sheer murder, and it is surprising that none of the senior officers on board did not themselves take action to release the men.

The object of Edwards' mission was to 'prevent the mutineers from escaping, having proper regard to the preservation of their lives, that they may be brought home to undergo the punishment due to their demerits'. It seems clear that Edwards did not have proper regard to the preservation of their lives, and showed a wicked and wanton disregard which, in all the circumstances, was totally inexcusable.

Another aspect of his management of affairs during the crisis of the shipwreck seems highly questionable. This shipwreck was a prolonged and agonizing affair. The *Pandora* did not founder for eleven or twelve hours after she struck. There were thus several hours in which to stock up the boats with food, stores and water, especially water, and utensils in which to carry it.

Edwards knew that a prolonged boat voyage in tropical waters under a burning sun lay ahead; he knew that nearly one hundred men had to be provided for, and that the common fate of castaways in open boats was severe privation from hunger and thirst. Yet according to the scanty allowances on which the survivors had to exist, and according to Heywood, and to Morrison's and the surgeon's accounts, no more than two or three bags of bread (ship's biscuit) two or three beakers of water and a little wine were put in the boats.

Edwards had much to preoccupy him during this time, but what were his officers doing?

There was Mr Edmonds, the captain's clerk; there was Mr George Hamilton, the surgeon; there was Mr Gregory Bentham, the purser, a very experienced purser who had sailed with Captain Cook, and there was Mr Cherry, praised by the surgeon 'for his uncommon attention to the victualling during the voyage'.

What were all these experienced people doing all this time?

Surgeon Hamilton did not attempt to explain. All he wrote was: 'Providentially a small barrel of water, a cag of wine, some biscuit and a few muskets, had been thrown into the boat. The heat of the sun and the reflection from the sand was now excruciating.'

They had been warned, but they do not seem to have heeded the warning. Even Captain Edwards himself remarks in his Report to the Admiralty: 'Our boats were kept astern of the ship and a small quantity of provisions and other necessaries were put into them.'

Captain Edwards also stated that 'when the ship beat over the reef, we had ten fathoms of water', i.e. sixty feet, in which the *Pandora* foundered. As she lay on her side, the wreck was completely covered by water, but clearly visible below. On the following day, a boat was sent to the wreck to see if anything could be procured, but with the exception of some rigging and a chain, they found not a single article of food. The boat was also sent fishing but caught nothing at all.

When the *Pandora* sank, the four boats were busy picking up the men in the water. They then made for a small island or cay which was seen four miles from the wreck. Here everybody was mustered and it was found that eighty-nine of the *Pandora*'s company were saved and ten of the 'pirates', and that thirty-one of the ship's company were lost and four 'pirates'. An account was made of the available food and water, and all hands were put on a daily allowance; three ounces of bread, half an ounce of portable soup, half an ounce of essence of malt, two small glasses of water and one of wine.

Surgeon Hamilton complained of the

excruciating heat and the reflection from the sand; our stomachs being filled with salt water from the great length of time we were swimming rendered our thirst most intolerable and no water was allowed to be served out the first day. We found we could admit an allowance of two small wine glasses of water daily to each man for sixteen days. A saw and hammer had fortunately been found in a boat which enabled us to make preparations for the voyage by repairing one boat which was in a bad state and cutting up the floor boards of all the boats into uprights round which we stretched canvas to keep the water from breaking on board, and we made tents of the boats' sails. When it was dark, we set the watch and went to sleep. In the night we were disturbed by one of the men, Connell, which led us to suspect he had got at the wine but on further enquiry we found the torture he suffered from thirst led him to drink salt water by which means he went mad and died in the sequel of the voyage.

Next morning, some of the gigantic cockle was boiled and cut into junks lest anyone should be inclined to eat but our thirst was too excessive to bear anything which would increase it. This evening a wine glass of water was served to each man. A paper parcel of tea having been thrown into the boat, the officers joined all their allowance and had tea in the captain's tent with him. When it was boiled, everyone took a salt cellar spoonful and passed it to his neighbour by which means we moisted our mouths by slow degrees and received much refreshment from it.

The *Pandora* sank in the early morning of 29 August. Next day the survivors were busy sorting themselves out and preparing the boats. No time was lost. At half-past ten on 31 August, the flotilla of four boats set forth. The destination was Timor, 1,100 miles away. Each boat was given the latitude and longitude of Timor. The order of sailing was as follows:

PINNACE — Capt. Edwards, Lieut. Hayward, 19 men and three prisoners.

RED YAWL — First Lieut. John Larkan, Geo. Hamilton the surgeon, twenty-one men and two prisoners.

LAUNCH — Lieut. Corner, Gregory Bentham the Purser, twenty-three men and two prisoners.

BLUE YAWL — Mr Geo. Passmore the Master, nineteen men and three prisoners.

Captain Edwards viewed the mutineers, even in these altered circumstances, with suspicion. In his Journal, Morrison wrote a detailed account of the stay on the sand cay:

A tent was set up for the officers and another for the men, but we were not suffered to come near either, tho the captain had told us we should be used as well as the ships company but we found that was not the case. On requesting the captain for a spare boats sail to shelter us from the sun (being mostly naked) it was refused, tho no use was made of it. We were ordered to keep on a part of the island by ourselves, to windward of the tents, not being suffered to speak to any person but each other; the provision saved being very small, this days allowance was only a mouthful of bread and a glass of wine, the water being but a small quantity, none could be afforded.

We staid here till Wednesday morning the 31st,[1] fitting the boats, during which time the sun took such an effect on us, who had been cooped up for five months, that we had our skin flea'd off from head to foot, tho we kept ourselves covered in the sand during the day.

[1] Morrison's accuracy regarding exact dates and other details is remarkable. No doubt he got these details from Bligh's and Hamilton's books.

Chapter 22

The Boat Voyage

Now began one of those stern endurance tests, a boat voyage rivalling any of the famous boat voyages of the past, but lacking the accompanying publicity.

In some respects, Edwards' boat voyage was more remarkable even than Bligh's. When Bligh and his men were forced into the boat, they were fat, well nourished and spoiled by six months' glorious holidays (and for most of them honeymoons) in Tahiti. Edwards and his men had just endured three days of agonizing mental and physical trials. Bligh had eighteen men only to consider; Edwards had Ninety and Nine. Bligh's party suffered from hunger; Edwards' men experienced the worse tortures of thirst; Bligh's men could not keep warm; Edwards' men were burned by the sun. Bligh had one overloaded boat; Edwards had four, similarly overburdened. Bligh's odyssey was more prolonged than Edwards'; Bligh had to find his own way; Edwards had a copy of Bligh's home-made chart. Bligh missed Endeavour Strait thinking it a Bay of Islands; Edwards, following Bligh, missed it also. Bligh relied on rum to keep his men alive; Edwards had a small quantity of wine. Both Bligh and Edwards found that the younger men bore the physical privations better than the older men, but each noted the 'excessive irritability' caused by their sufferings. Both parties caught booby birds, sucked their blood and divided them into small portions. To make more room in his boat, Bligh placed his men on watch and watch, so that half were lying down and half were sitting up alternately. Edwards adopted a different plan. Seeing that his four boats would be overcrowded, 'we laid the oars upon the thwarts which formed a platform by which means we stowed two tiers of men'.

Neither party seems to have been very successful in catching fish, but both consumed a great deal of shell fish (giant cockles).

Bligh had another advantage over Edwards. He was only thirty-five years of age at the time, whereas Edwards was in his fiftieth year. Though Bligh undoubtedly suffered a severe emotional shock on the morning of the mutiny, it was all over in an hour, but Edwards' ordeal lasted for two or more days and the ordeal must have been at least as severe as, if not greater than, that suffered by the younger man.

There is one further difference between the two commanders. On his safe return to England, Bligh was hailed as a hero and the ensuing publicity was greatly enhanced by the early publication of his *Narrative*, in which he detailed at great length a day-to-day account of the boat voyage.

The return to England of Edwards and his ship's company seems to have attracted little or no publicity. What publicity there was was concerned with two matters which had nothing to do with the *Pandora*, or at least was only indirectly related to that ship and her company.

This may have been partly due to the fact that unlike Bligh, Captain Edwards was not a ready writer. He had no itch to publicize his exploits and adventures. As Sir Basil Thomson complained: 'He did not take a place in the front rank of the literature of travel.'

He left that to others and it was Surgeon Hamilton who wrote the story of the *Pandora*'s voyage. Unlike Bligh's story, however, this small undistinguished volume had little or no publicity. Printed in a small provincial town (Berwick) in 1793 in a very limited edition, it seems to have passed unnoticed into obscurity, and nowadays is a 'rare and scarce' item in booksellers' catalogues, highly priced.

Captain Edwards indeed seems to have been altogether too modest and reticent. His description of his boat voyage is limited to the following:

It is unnecessary to retail our particular sufferings in the boats during the run to Timor. Sufficient to observe that we suffered more from heat and thirst than from hunger and that our strength was greatly decreased. At seven o'clock in the morning of the 13th September we saw the island of Timor bearing N.W.

So much for that.

Surgeon Hamilton's account is in greater detail. After narrating how they followed Bligh's track to the northwards seeking a way to Torres Strait, he wrote:

We came to an inhabited island from which we promised ourselves a supply of water. The natives flocked down to the beach in crowds. They were jet black and neither sex had either covering or girdle. We made signals of distress to them for something to drink, which they understood; on receiving some trifling presents of knives and some buttons cut from our coats, they brought us a cag of good water which we emptied and sent it back to be filled again. They would not bring it a second time but put it down on the beach and made signs for us to come for it.

This we declined as we observed the women and children running and supplying the men with bows and arrows. They let fly a shower of arrows among the thick of us. Luckily we had not a man wounded, but an arrow fell between the captain and third lieutenant (Hayward) and went through the thwart and stuck in it. It was an oak plank inch thick. We discharged a volley of muskets at them which put them to flight, but none killed.

We steered from these hostile savages to other islands in sight and sent some armed men on shore (to look for water) with orders to keep pretty near us, but they returned without success.

In the evening we steered for those islands which we supposed were called the Prince of Wales's Islands, named by Captain Cook and before midnight came to a grapnel near one of these islands, in a large sound formed by the surrounding islands. We named it Sandwich Sound.[1]

It is fit for the reception of ships, there is plenty of wood and by digging we found very good water. We saw several wolves near the watering place[2] but no natives. Here we filled our vessels with water. After having gorged our parched bodies with water, till we were perfectly water-logged, we began to feel the cravings of hunger; a new sensation of misery we had hitherto been strangers to, from the excess of thirst predominating. Some of our stragglers were lucky enough to find a few small oysters and some berrys. We carefully avoided shooting at any bird lest the report of the muskets should alarm the natives. Centinels were placed to prevent stragglers of our party and when every other thing was filled with water, the carpenter's boots were also filled. The water in them was first served out, on account of leakage.

This place is extremely well situated for a rendezvous in surveying Endeavour Straits; and were a little colony settled here, a concatenation of Christian settlements would enchain the world and be useful to any unfortunate ship that might be wrecked in these seas; or should a rupture take place in South America, a great vein of commerce might find its way through this channel.[3]

In the evening we saw the northern extremity of New South Wales (Cape York) which forms the south side of Endeavour Strait. At night, the boats took each other in tow, and we steered to the Westward, and entered the great Indian Ocean.

This was the evening of 2 September, sixty hours from the time the flotilla of boats had set out from Wreck Cay. During that time Captain Edwards had successfully navigated his little fleet through the archipelago surrounding Torres Strait, had managed to avoid any battles with the hostile savages and had found some water with which they had filled every container. Surgeon Hamilton wrote:

We now had a voyage of a thousand miles to undertake in our open boats. As soon

[1] This was the Prince of Wales' Channel or Flinders Channel, first traversed by Bligh and now followed by Edwards, both in light draft boats.

[2] Dingoes.

[3] A 'great vein of commerce' nowadays does find its way through this channel, and the little colony established on Thursday Island.

as we cleared the land, we found a very heavy swell running, which threatened destruction to our little fleet; for should we have separated, we must inevitably perish for want of water, as we had not utensils to divide our slender stock. For our mutual preservation we took each other in tow, but the sea was so rough, and the swell running so high, we towed very hard, and broke a new tow line. This put us in the utmost confusion, being afraid of dashing to pieces upon each other, as it was a very dark night. We again made fast to each other, but the tow line breaking a second time, we were obliged to trust ourselves to the mercy of the waves.

At five in the morning the pinnace (Captain Edwards' boat) lay to, as the other boats had passed her under a dark cloud; but on the signal being made for the boats to join, we again met at daylight. At noon we passed some remarkable black and yellow striped sea snakes.

4th September. Gave out the exact latitude of our rendezvous in writing; also the longitude by the timekeeper at this present time, in case of unavoidable separation.

This is interesting for several reasons. It shows that in all the excitement and confusion of leaving the wrecked ship, someone – presumably the navigator (Lieut. Hayward) and the master (George Passmore) – had remembered to put in the boats the valuable chronometer and Bligh's chart. In the run from Torres Strait to Timor, the latitude did not vary at all. The course was due west, along the parallel of 10° S.

In each boat there were two officers who were quite familiar with this simple fact and would not need to be told 'the exact latitude of our rendezvous' (Coupang). As for the longitude, it enabled them to know the speed of their progress westerly and also warn them when they were near or on the meridian of Coupang so that they did not pass it unawares in the dark.

Hamilton continues:

On the night of 5–6th September, the sea running very cross and high, the tow line broke several times, the boats strained and made much water, and we were obliged to leave off towing the rest of the voyage, or it would have dragged the boats asunder.

On the 7th, the captain's boat caught a booby; they sucked his blood and divided him into twenty four shares.

The men who were employed steering the boats were often subject to a *coup de soleil*, as everyone else were continually wetting their shirts overboard and putting it upon their head, which alleviated the scorching heat of the sun to which we were entirely exposed, most of us having lost our hats while swimming at the time the ship was wrecked. It may be observed that this method of wetting our bodies with salt water is not advisable if the misery is protracted beyond three or four days, as after that time the great absorption from the skin that takes place from the increased heat and fever makes the fluids become tainted with the bitter of the salt water; so much so that the saliva became intolerable in the mouth.

It may likewise be worthy of remark that those who drank their own urine died in the sequel of the voyage.

Our mouths were so parched that few attempted to eat and what was not claimed was thrown into the general stock. We found the old people suffer much more than those who were young. A particular instance we observed in one young boy, a midshipman, young Matson who sold his allowance of water two days for one allowance of bread. As their sufferings continued, they became very cross and savage in their temper. In the captain's boat, one of the prisoners took to praying and they gathered round him with much attention and seeming devotion. But the captain suspecting the purity of his doctrines and unwilling he should make a monopoly of the business gave prayers himself.[1]

It is not difficult to comprehend the physical and mental condition of the people in the boats. Captain Edwards himself must have been in a very depressed state. He was in his fiftieth year, no longer tough and resilient. He had just lost his ship, and some lives had been lost too. He was only too well aware of the hardships now confronting him and his men, and a sense of failure possessed him.

The physical condition of his men was deplorable. Anyone who has spent even an idle day in an open boat under a hot sun with the glare and the salt spray and the hard thwarts and with plenty of room to move about and to stretch the limbs will be aware of the stiffness, the sunburn and the feeling of general discomfort at the end of the day.

The men of the *Pandora* were weary, sick, sore, thirsty, clad in rags, unable to move and uncertain of what the morrow might bring forth. There was absolutely no possible chance of help for them. There were no passing ships and no signals of distress could help them. They reeled to and fro and staggered like drunken men and were veritably at their wit's end.

Ahead of them lay open sea, surrounded by lands and islands from which on any day at any moment savage barbarians might issue forth to the attack in fast sailing canoes, armed with poisoned arrows and spears. Not to mention bad weather and the ever-present probability of boat or boats being overwhelmed and sunk.

Here again the irrepressible diarist, James Morrison, makes his comments. No gales, mutinies, boat voyages or handcuffs could avail to prevent him sedulously inditing his observations, notes and reflections on current affairs. He may have been deprived of everything he possessed by an unfeeling captain and officers, but not his daily Journal.

[1] This was presumably James Morrison.

The Boat Voyage

Here is the Journal again, in the pinnace in the middle of the Arafura Sea, with Captain Edwards, Lieut. Hayward, Mr Rickards, master's mate, Mr Packer, gunner, Mr Edmonds, the captain's clerk, sixteen Marine privates, McIntosh, young Ellison, and Morrison himself. All very thirsty, all very stiff and sore, all weak and ill, all cross and savage in their temper, 'dipping our finger in the water and wetting our mouths by slow degrees'.

Nevertheless, Morrison remembered every detail, even the day, the date:

On the 9th [September] I was laying on the oars talking to McIntosh when Captn. Edwards ordered me aft. Without assigning any cause, he ordered me to be pinnioned with a cord and lassh'd down in the boat's bottom. Ellison who was then asleep in the boat's bottom was ordered to the same punishment.[1]

I attempted to reason and enquire what I had now done to be thus cruelly treated, urging the distress'd situation of the whole, but received for answer, 'Silence, you murdering villain – are you not a prisoner? You piratical dog, what better treatment do you expect?'

I then told him that it was a disgrace to the captain of a British man o' war to treat a prisoner in such an inhuman manner, upon which he started up in a violent rage, and snatching a pistol which lay in the stern sheets threatened to shoot me. I still attempted to speak, when he swore 'By God! if you speak another word I'll heave the log with you!'

Finding that he would hear no reason and my mouth being parched so that I could not move my tongue, I was forced to be silent and submit; and was tyed down so that I could not move.

In this miserable situation, Ellison and I remained for the rest of the passage, nor was McIntosh suffered to come near or speak to either of us.

Unfortunately, Morrison is the only witness to this deplorable action by the captain. There is no other evidence whatever, and we have therefore to rely upon his word, and his word only.

Apparently, Captain Edwards regarded Morrison with a peculiar dislike but it is not clear why. Morrison seems to have irritated him for some reason or other, and Hamilton records that in the boat 'everyone was very cross and savage in their temper'. There were twenty-four people in the boat. Why pick on Morrison? Morrison, with lamb-like innocence, says 'I was laying on the oars talking to McIntosh,' which was hardly sufficient cause to rouse the captain to a fury. Was he perhaps the prisoner who 'took to praying', the prisoner round whom the others gathered with much attention and seeming devotion?

[1] Tom Ellison though rated Able Seaman was only seventeen years of age.

Following him, Owen Rutter echoes Sir Basil Thomson's opinion of Morrison when he says: 'There is no doubt that he was a bit of a sea lawyer.'

Dr George Mackaness contents himself with saying: 'Of the man himself and the authenticity of his Diary (as he himself named it) the most divergent opinions have been held.'

Sir William Laird Clowes stated: 'Morrison was a man of good character . . . a witness that can be trusted.'[1]

These divergent views make it difficult to penetrate the character of the man. One thing seems clear – he was not a revolutionary, or a rebel, or a mutineer, as is shown by his opinion of the officers of the *Bounty* during the mutiny: 'The behaviour of the officers on this occasion was dastardly beyond description, none of them even making the least attempt to rescue the ship which would have been effected had any attempt been made by one of them. . . .' thus clearly revealing himself on the side of law, order and authority. But he was a radical, for ever sticking up for his rights, a shop-steward before the days of unions, for ever demanding his pound, his pint and his right, a man before his time. Already, he had been through an exhausting, harassing time, ever since he had been incarcerated in the *Pandora*. This was the very nadir of his fortunes. He had been in irons during April, May, June, July and August; he had been very near to death, and was still in a hazardous situation; he had suffered and was suffering the pangs of thirst and hunger, the sores and bruises and physical discomforts of his environment. His future offered little hope. At the best, he would arrive back in England a broken and penniless man, with not a penny of pay due to him; at the worst, he would be hanged. Now, he lay in the bottom of the boat, bound, in abject misery, physical and mental. Yet the fellow continued to stand up for his rights, and when he attempted to reason with the captain and to appeal to the Rights of Man, he was branded a piratical dog.

His sole asset was his so-called 'Diary', his poor miserable manuscript, sedulously written up from day to day, still preserved, we are told, as he lay bound in the bottom of the boat. If this was all he possessed, Morrison was poor indeed. What literary agent or publisher would consider such a manuscript? And if he contemplated remaining in the Service, his only calling, could it be published, with its reflections on and its criticisms of two of his captains? Had this Journal been confiscated by Captain Edwards and handed to the prosecution at Morrison's trial, he could hardly have escaped being hanged, particularly as he had acted as bo'sun for the mutineers in the *Bounty* after the mutiny.

[1] Clowes, *The Royal Navy*, vol. IV, p. 102.

Yet what a tale he had to tell! This was no travel on life's common way, but along a most uncommon way. This was almost as good as Robinson Crusoe. It was a genuine story, no fake, no fiction, no Trader Horn, no Munchausen. It was a round unvarnished tale of moving accidents by flood and field, of blood, cannibals, wreck, love, hells and heavens.

And it contained a minute and detailed account of the life and customs of the people of Tahiti, then still largely unknown, and still a popular attraction as the island of free love.

For nearly half a century, the Morrison MS has reposed in the Mitchell Library in Sydney, a treasured relic and record of the mutiny of the *Bounty* and the voyage of the *Pandora*.

Morrison need not repine, if his spirit still lingers in his vast and wandering grave, known only to God. Whatever his literary aspirations, they were fulfilled and even exceeded in 1935 by a discerning publisher, the Golden Cockerel Press, in the person of the late Owen Rutter who printed his Journal from the original with the permission and approval of the Library Trustees.

It was produced in a style which Morrison could not have conceived possible, printed on mould-made paper in black and green, in full morocco, decorated with engravings and priced at twenty guineas a copy, or in more modest binding at four guineas. In this gallery of de luxe volumes Morrison strikes a bizarre note but a not unworthy one, even if his so-called Journal is a misleading label on a genuine document.

Genuine, but could it be contemporary? 'In this miserable situation I remained for the rest of the passage' and in that miserable situation, 'bound and tyed so that I could not move,' how did he continue to write up his daily diary, let alone preserve it?

Chapter 23

Arrival at Coupang

THE boats sailed on. The days passed. Surgeon Hamilton wrote:

On the 9th September we passed a great many of the Nautilus fish, the shell of which served us to put our glass of water into, by which means we had more time granted to dip our finger in it, and set our mouths by slow degrees. There were several flocks of birds seen flying in a direction for the land.

Four days later when their misery was past bearing and this highly disciplined grim little armada was nearing the end of its tether, the end of the passage hove in sight!

On the 13th in the morning, we saw land. The discoverer was immediately rewarded with a glass of water; but as if our cup of misery was not completely full, it fell a dead calm.

The boats now all separated, every one pushing to make the land. Next day we got pretty near the land, but there was a prodigious surf running. Two of our men slung a bottle about their necks, jumped overboard and swam through the surf. They traversed over a good many miles till a creek intercepted them, when they came down to the beach and made signs to us of their not having succeeded. We then brought the boat as near the surf as we durst venture, and picked them up.

In running along the coast, about twelve o'clock, we had the pleasure to see the red yawl get into a creek. She had hoisted an English jack at her masthead, that we might observe her in running down the coast. There was a prodigious surf and many dangerous shoals between us and the mouth of the creek. We however began to share the remains of our water and about half a bottle came to each man's share which we dispatched in an instant.

We now gained fresh spirits and hazarded everything in gaining our so-much-wished-for haven. It is but justice here to acknowledge how much we were indebted to the intrepidity, courage, and seamanlike behaviour of Mr. Reynolds the master's mate who fairly beat her over all the reefs and brought us safe on shore. The crew of the blue yawl who had been two or three hours landed assisted in landing our party. A fine spring of water near to the creek afforded us immediate relief. As soon as we had filled our bellys, a guard was placed over the prisoners and we went to sleep for a few hours on the grass.

In the afternoon a Chinese chief came down the creek in a canoe, attended by some of the natives, to wait upon us. He was a venerable looking old man; we endeavoured to walk down to the waterside to receive him, and acquaint him with the nature of our distress.

We addressed him in French and in English, neither of which he understood, but misery was so strongly depicted in our countenance that language was superfluous. The tears trickling down his venerable cheeks convinced us he saw and felt our misfortunes, and silence was eloquence on the subject. He made us understand by signs that without fee or reward, we should be supplied with horses and conducted to Coupang, a Dutch East India settlement, about seventy mile distant, the place of our rendezvous. This we politely declined, as the nature of our duty in the charge of the prisoners would not admit of it. We took leave of him for the present, after receiving promises of refreshment.

Soon after, crowds of the natives came down with fowls, pigs, milk and bread. Mr Innes, the surgeon's mate happened to have some silver in his pocket to which they applied the touchstone, but they would not give us anything for our guineas. However, anchor buttons answered the purpose, as they gave us provisions for a few buttons which they refused the same number of guineas for, till a hungry dog [man] one of the carpenter's crew, happening to pick up an officer's jacket spoiled the market by giving it, buttons and all for a pair of fowls which a few buttons might have purchased.

All hands were busied in roasting the fowls and boiling the pork and in the evening we made a very hearty supper. While we were regaling ourselves round a large fire, some wild beast gave a roar in the bushes. Some who had been in India before declared it was the jackall; we therefore concluded the lion could not be far off. Some were jocularly observing what a glorious supper the lord of the forest would make of us, but others were rather troubled with the dismaloes. This gave a gloomy turn to the conversation and with our minds having been previously much engaged with savages and wild beasts, and our bodies worn out through famine and watching, I believe the contagious effects of fear became pretty general.

From Bligh's narrative and others, we had been warned of the danger of landing in any other part of the island of Timor but Coupang, the Dutch settlement, as they were represented hostile and savage.

Next day we went up the creek in one of the boats about four miles to one of their towns to purchase provisions for our sea store. In purchasing a pig the man, finding a good price for it, offered to traffic with us for the charms of his daughter, a very pretty young girl. But none of us seemed inclined that way, as there were many good things we stood much more in need of.

At one o'clock we embarked in our boats for Coupang. We sailed along the coast all day until it was dark.

At daybreak we again proceeded on our voyage, and at five in the afternoon, we landed at Coupang.

The Governor, Mynheer Vanion[1] received us with the utmost politeness, kindness and hospitality. The Lieutenant Governor was equally kind and attentive in giving the necessary orders for our support and relief in our present distressed state.

Next morning being Sunday as we supposed, the 17th September we were preparing for Church to return thanks to Almighty God but were disappointed in our pious intentions. We found it was Monday the 18th, having lost a day by performing a circuit of the globe to the westward.

They had arrived, but only at World's End. Coupang was the last outpost of western Christendom beyond which was uttermost darkness. It was the last port of call and the first port of refuge. It was the Ultima Thule of the Orient for which all travellers and explorers made in search of aid and comfort.

Captain Cook put in here on his First Voyage in the *Endeavour Bark* seeking rest and refreshment. Captain Bligh had made unerringly for Coupang; so too had Captain Edwards.

Long before any of them, however, had come Captain Dampier in HMS *Roebuck*, the first Englishman and the first of the King's ships to sail in these waters and to visit these lands, one hundred years before:

And thus having ranged about a considerable time upon this [New Holland] coast without finding any good fresh water or any convenient place to clean the ship as I had hoped for; and it being moreover the height of the dry season, and my men growing Scorbutick for want of Refreshments, so that I had little incouragement to search further, I resolved to leave this coast and accordingly in the beginning of September 1699, I set sail toward Timor.[2]

The Dutch were jealous and suspicious of the English ship's arrival and the Governor sent an officer to enquire what Dampier was doing there and invited him to dine with him. 'There was plenty of very good victuals and well drest; and the Linnen was white and clean and all the Dishes and Plates of Silver or fine China' recorded the appreciative Dampier.

Having cleaned his ship and restocked his water and provisions, he sailed in December 1699 bound for the unknown East, and the discovery of New Britain. This discovery and naming of 'New Britain' projected the English flag to the furthermost corner of the globe.

These young mariners of a now ancient past had no illusions of heroism

---

[1] Variously spelt Van John, Vanjon, Vanion, Wanjon. He had resided as Resident Governor in Coupang for some years, having married the daughter of his predecessor, Willem Adrian van Este who was Governor when the *Bounty*'s launch arrived in June 1789, more than two years before.

[2] Dampier. *Collection of Voyages.*

or grandeur. There was no Tennysonian *Ulysses* among them pining to sail beyond the sunset and the baths of all the western stars until they died. Nor was there a single representative of the Press to 'write them up'. According to Captain Edwards, there was nothing to write home about.

Edwards landed at Coupang with his party of shipwrecked people for whom he desired immediate accommodation. The church and the churchyard were assigned by the Governor for the use of the crew, a house was taken for the warrant and petty officers, and the ship's officers were the guests of the Dutch officers and officials, the captain being the guest of the Governor. Everybody was very kind to everybody, but from this general benevolence the 'pirates' were excluded. They were confined in irons in Coupang Castle or Fort and fed on bad provisions.

Edwards and party remained at Coupang for three weeks recuperating and preparing for their homeward journey. Arrangements were made for the whole party to embark in the Dutch East Indiaman *Rembang* which was to take them to Batavia.

But before sailing Captain Edwards received a surprising and annoying piece of information. His large party of distressed British seamen and mutineers was to be further augmented.

Chapter 24

The Schooner Found

IT seems there was another party of British people awaiting passage to England, a party of eight men, a young woman and her two small children.

They had arrived at Coupang in a boat some weeks before Edwards' party and had informed the Governor that they were the survivors of an English brig, wrecked in these seas. The Governor attended to their every want and they drew bills on the British Government for which they were supplied with every necessity. But suspicion fell upon their bona fides and Surgeon Hamilton tells the real story of this strange group of adventurers.

It seems they were not the survivors of an English brig at all.

About a fortnight before we arrived at Coupang, a boat with eight men, a woman and two children came on shore here.

They told the Governor they were the supercargo, part of the crew and passengers of an English brig, wrecked in these seas.

His house, which has ever been the asylum of the distressed, was open for their reception, they drew Bills on the British Government and were supplied with every necessary.

The Captain of a Dutch East Indiaman who spoke English, hearing of the arrival of Captain Edwards and our unfortunate boats ran to them with the glad tidings of their captain having arrived.

But one of them, starting up in surprise, cried: What Captain? Dam'me, we have no captain!

For they had reported that the captain and remainder of the crew of the English brig had separated from them in other boats.

This immediately led to a suspicion of their being impostors and they were ordered to be apprehended and put into the castle. One of the men, and the woman fled into the woods but were soon taken. They then confessed they were English convicts, and that they had made their escape from Botany Bay in New Holland. They had been supplied with a quadrant, a compass, a chart from a Dutch ship that lay in Botany Bay and the expedition was conducted by their leader, one Will Bryant a fisherman from Cornwall, whose time of transportation he claimed, was expired. He was a good seaman and a tolerable navigator. They dragged along the coast of New South Wales in their boat and as often as the hostile nature of the savage natives would permit, hauled their boat up at night and slept on shore.

They met with several curious and interesting anecdotes in this voyage. In many places of the coast of South Wales, they found very good coal, a circumstance that was not before known.

The heroine of this boat voyage was the woman Mary Bryant, wife of William Bryant, the leader of the party. Her baptismal certificate reads:

Mary, daughter of William Broad, Mariner, and Grace his wife, of Fowey, was baptized in this Church on 1 May 1765 by Nicholas Cory, Vicar
(Fowey Parish Church Register).

She was therefore twenty-six when she made the boat voyage, with her two infants. One of these children, the elder, was apparently illegitimate since she was born in the convict transport *Charlotte* (and named Charlotte) when Mary Broad was on her way out to Botany Bay. She was married to William Bryant after arriving there. A second child Emanuel was born at Botany Bay and was still an infant in arms when they set out in the boat for Timor.

In their journey, the escaped convicts had sailed and rowed their six-oared boat a distance of 3,254 miles, taking sixty-nine days.

They had achieved this unique feat without losing a single member of the party, although one was a baby at the breast. Unschooled, unlearned, unlettered, they had navigated an open boat along 2,000 miles of unknown coastline, through a coral archipelago of 1,000 miles, and then crossed 1,200 miles of trackless sea.

As a sustained feat of seamanship and endurance their boat voyage equalled if it did not excel those of Bligh and Edwards. Whereas their boat parties yearned to be homeward-bound, the escaped convicts were fugitives with no home awaiting them.[1]

Preparations were now complete for the embarkation of all hands in the Dutch ship *Rembang*. Captain Edwards signed bills for the food and other necessaries supplied by the Dutch authorities for maintenance and clothing for the convicts, all of whom, except the woman, were in irons. The *Pandora*'s boats were sold and on 6 October 1791, the *Rembang* sailed from Coupang bound for Batavia. The route lay via Allas Strait and along the north coast of Java to Samarang. Daily at 4 p.m. the convicts and mutineers were unchained and brought up on deck for air and necessary functions. An hour later they were taken below and chained up for the

[1] For a full account see *The Strange Case of Mary Bryant* by G. Rawson. London, 1935.

night. Captain Edwards had no reason to fear further plottings. Neither the mutineers nor the convicts were in any condition to fight again. With their health partially or permanently undermined and suffering from dejection, they thought only of an early end to their suffering and the stoutest-hearted were sunk in lethargy. Even Morrison's voice was no longer heard. The convicts' leader, William Bryant, seemed to be sinking and Surgeon Hamilton visited him daily, but Captain Edwards' attitude was summed up in the phrase: 'The only good convict is a dead one.'

When a tropical storm fell upon the *Rembang*, the hatches were closed as the seas swept on board and flooded the 'tween decks. Unable to move, pirates and convicts lay chilled and miserable in the darkness. The woman convict, Mary Bryant, strove to keep her ailing husband and babies dry as the vessel heeled and rolled and the roar of the storm drowned the cries of the children.

Next morning Bali was in sight, the storm abated and the master of the *Rembang* entered in his logbook: 'Gale abated. English sailors assist our men. Breeze strong from East. Made sail. Bali in sight on port beam.'

The short passage from Coupang to Samarang was seriously delayed by adverse winds, calms and gales. The *Rembang* had sailed from Coupang on 6 October. It was not until 30 October that she anchored in Samarang harbour.

And here, not only Captain Edwards but all hands met with a pleasing and astonishing surprise.

There before them, peacefully at anchor, was the stout little vessel, the schooner *Resolution*, long since given up for lost.

Chapter 25

The Schooner's Tale

CAPTAIN EDWARDS reported this gratifying incident with his customary phlegm.

We stopped at Samarang where we had the good fortune to be joined by our tender, *Resolution*, that had separated from us off the island of Oattoah. She had all her people on board except one man whom they had buried a few days before. She had been stopped here on suspicion and they were going to send her to Batavia. Mr. Overstratin, the Governor of this place, delivered her up to me. She had contracted a small debt for provisions which I shall discharge.

Surgeon Hamilton was a little more effusive:

Immediately on our coming to anchor, we were agreeably surprised to find our tender here, which we had so long given up for lost. Never was social affection more eminently pourtrayed than in the meeting of these poor fellows; and from excess of joy, and a recital of their mutual sufferings, from pestilence, famine and shipwreck, a flood of tears filled every man's breast.

It seems from the account given by Edwards and Hamilton (there being no other narrative of this remarkable adventure) that on the night of 22 June 1791, when the *Pandora* lost sight of the schooner in a rain-squall off the island of Upolu that the natives made a determined attack from canoes. Never having seen firearms and not understanding the connection between the reports of the guns and the fall of their fellows, they maintained the attack with great fury, endeavouring to board the schooner and slaughter the crew of nine. But for the boarding netting they would easily have taken the vessel; one man succeeding in scrambling on board and would have felled the captain, Oliver, with his club had he not been shot dead at the moment of striking.

Oliver's situation at this time was serious. He had beaten off one attack but would certainly have to face others if he remained in the vicinity. At the same time he was very short of water and food which was actually due to be delivered to him by the *Pandora* that morning. The *Pandora*, however,

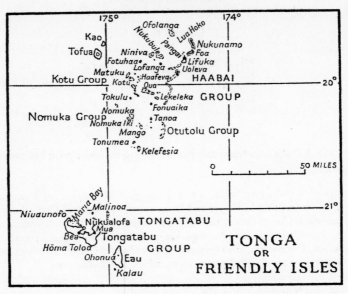

was not in sight, the people of Upolu were not to be trusted and he could not risk landing for food and water. During all that day and all the next he remained cruising in the vicinity, keeping a sharp lookout for the frigate.

At length in desperate need of food and water, he decided to make for the appointed rendezvous at Anamooka,[1] 360 miles due south of Upolu. 360 miles was not a great distance for the fast sailing schooner. At an average of six knots, she would have reached Anamooka in sixty hours.

But apparently the passage took much longer, for having drunk their last drop of water they suffered torture from thirst. So much so that young Renouard the midshipman became delirious and continued very ill for some weeks, an additional anxiety for Oliver. They evidently experienced more leeway than Oliver allowed for and this, combined with a current setting to the westward, drifted them away to the west. When at last they sighted land they thought it was Anamooka. In point of fact it was Tofoa, lying north-west of Nomuka.

Arrived at Tofoa and thinking he was at Anamooka, in desperate need of water and food, Oliver opened trade with the natives who gave them water and provisions in return for iron nails. Having lulled the crew by

[1] The modern name is Nomuka.

this peaceful trading, the people of Tofoa, like the people of Upolu, made a sudden attack in an attempt to overpower the men and seize the schooner. Once again the Nine beat them off with their fire-power. The *Resolution* like Drake's *Golden Hind* was a veritable Spitfire.

While this desperate battle was in progress at Tofoa, Edwards lay unsuspectingly at Anamooka. With a south-easterly breeze the guns of the *Pandora* could have been heard by the schooner's people; with a good glass the masts of the frigate might have been visible from the schooner. Had Edwards approached the Anamooka archipelago on the west side instead of the east, he would probably have sighted the schooner and passed near Tofoa. In daylight, the crew of the schooner would, in that case, almost certainly have sighted the tall masts and sails of the frigate and by night 'the burning mountain on Tofoa exhibited a very grand spectacle' and would have drawn all eyes in the frigate to the island where the schooner lay.

But such was the irony of circumstance that neither frigate nor schooner suspected the close presence of the other.

Like Captain Bligh whose boat party had been so viciously attacked by the Tofoans, Oliver considered it too risky to remain there a moment longer than was necessary. Within twenty-four hours of his arrival at Tofoa, he sailed away on 1 July into the unknown blue.

It was indeed into the unknown blue that Oliver sailed. There were several good reasons which must have impelled him to steer west. It was the nearest way home, or at least to the Dutch settlements. He knew Captain Edwards was bound for Endeavour Strait, and he either would be following the *Pandora* or preceding her. Endeavour Strait was an obvious rendezvous to make for, and finally the south-east trade wind was a fair wind for him. Furthermore, in his little craft he did not feel particularly safe among these savages and deceitful islanders, manned as she was by but six Marines, not yet 'Royal', a quartermaster and a very ill midshipman. And he was short of food and water.

Between Tofoa and Endeavour Strait there lay an almost completely unknown region extending over forty degrees of longitude. Within this vast area lay two important groups of islands, the New Hebrides and the Fiji Islands. Of these large archipelagoes, the New Hebrides had only recently been examined and surveyed, while the Fiji group, the most important in the whole of the South Pacific, remained practically unknown and wholly unexplored. Not only did Oliver have no idea of the existence of the Fiji Islands; he was unaware that they were inhabited by active cannibals.

Into this unknown danger area he now unwittingly steered, and his boldness or blindness was rewarded by a remarkable stroke of luck. After sailing 300 miles due west he came to an island, Matuku, one of the unknown Fiji group.

Oliver with his quartermaster, his six Marines and the very sick young midshipman Renouard needed rest and refreshment more than anything else.

They needed a safe haven where the natives would cease from troubling and the weary be at rest. Hitherto he had been chased from pillar to post. At Matuku he found a beautiful island where the natives lived in perpetual plenty, where there were streams of pure water, where the harbour gave complete safety for his small vessel, where the natives proved to be not cannibals but honest and hospitable, and where he was able to remain for no fewer than five weeks refitting and recuperating.[1]

In the course of these five weeks, Oliver's party had close intercourse with the natives, the first Europeans to do so. Oliver, without being aware of it, had stolen the thunder of the great men, Tasman, Cook, Vancouver, Bligh. Tasman had seen from a distance the northern extremity of the group; Cook had discovered an outlying island in the far south of the group, and Bligh, only a year before Edwards, had sailed in the *Bounty*'s launch right through the Feejees. 'I not only expected to have better weather but to see the Feejee Islands, as I have often understood from the natives that they lie in that direction. Captain Cook likewise considered them to be N.W. by W. from Tonga.'

But Bligh had been in no condition to do any exploring, being preoccupied among all his other troubles with keeping his boat afloat. Nevertheless, he made notes and drew some rough sketches and made the first running survey of the group, as he passed through.

Oliver's party were the first Europeans to land and communicate with the islanders, and HMS *Resolution* was the first European vessel to anchor in Fiji.

Now that they were rested, refreshed, revictualled and restored to health, Oliver continued his journey. The route from Matuku to Endeavour Strait took them through the New Hebrides where they most probably landed to replenish their water supply. Then with tireless persistence they began the long haul across the Coral Sea. Surgeon Hamilton recorded:

After much diversity of distress and similar encounters they at last made the reef that runs between New Guinea and New Holland, where the *Pandora* met her

[1] 'Where they had waited for me for five weeks.' Edwards' Report.

unhappy fate; and after traversing from shore to shore (i.e. from the New Guinea coast to the Queensland coast) without finding an opening, they were faced with the prospect of shipwreck or death by starvation, this intrepid young seaman boldly gave it the stem (i.e. headed directly for the reef) and beat over it.

Soon after they had passed through Endeavour Strait, they fell in with a small Dutch vessel who showed them every tenderness that the nature of their distress required.

Hamilton adds: 'They were soon landed at a small Dutch settlement.'

But what and where was this small Dutch settlement? Coupang was the furthest known outpost but evidently the Dutch authorities had by now established outposts even further east than Coupang. If so, these further extensions of Dutch influence must have been unknown to the British Government since neither Captain Cook, Captain Bligh nor Captain Edwards appears to have been informed of them. When they were all three in urgent need of relief, they all persisted in making for the far-distant Coupang when nearer European settlements were available. Where could the Dutch have established further settlements? On the east coast of Timor, or on what is now known as Arnhem Land, or on the south coast of New Guinea? Had the schooner been escorted to Coupang, Hamilton would have said so. He was very familiar with Coupang and with the Governor Mynheer Vanion. Furthermore, why was the schooner escorted not to the nearest port of call, Coupang, but to far-distant Samarang in Java, when Coupang actually lay en route?

In any case, when Oliver's party was landed at this 'small Dutch settlement' wherever it was located, the governor of that place received these honest British seamen with considerable suspicion. He had been informed by the authorities at Batavia, like all outlying Dutch stations, of the mutiny in the *Bounty* and Captain Bligh had requested the Dutch to keep a lookout for the mutineers. Now here was a small, recently built home-made vessel constructed of Polynesian timbers which, according to Oliver, had been sailed from Tahiti, of all places. As for Oliver himself, who and what was he? And his companions, midshipman Renouard, James Dodds, the quartermaster, and those six privates of Marines?

The Dutch governor seemed to be almost convinced that they were *Bounty* mutineers. Oliver being a mere petty officer had nothing to identify him as an officer, warrant officer, or even petty officer in the Royal Navy. He had only his bare *ipse dixit*, and that was not enough. The governor treated them kindly but placed a strict guard over them and in due course they were escorted to Samarang.

Pandora and *Resolution* had lost sight of each other on 22 June. They were not reunited until 30 October, more than four months later.

In view of the fact that he needed cash immediately with which to purchase clothing for his tattered crew and since he could not take the *Resolution* with him, even had he wished to, Captain Edwards put her up for auction at Samarang.

The price she fetched enabled the crew to be reclothed for the passage home, but young Peter Heywood complained bitterly later on that no clothing was given either to the mutineers or to the convicts, except what they could earn by plaiting and selling straw hats. How the woman convict and her two ailing infants fared for new clothes is not related.

Chapter 26

Homeward Bound

FROM Samarang the whole party proceeded to Batavia. Surgeon Hamilton wrote:

In a few days we arrived at Batavia, the emporeum of the Dutch in the East. Our first care was employed in sending to the hospital the sickly remains of our unfortunate crew. Some dead bodies floating down the canal struck our boat which had a very disagreeable effect on the minds of our brave fellows whose nerves were reduced to a very weak state from sickness. This was a *coup de grâce* to a sick man on his premier entrée into this painted sepulchre, this golgotha of Europe, which buries the whole settlement every five years.

Among those admitted to hospital was William Bryant, the convicts' leader, and the infant Emanuel. Captain Edwards had refused permission for Mrs Bryant to accompany her husband to hospital but some adverse remarks from one or other of the Dutch community reached his ears and he judged it expedient to make some show of magnanimity. The young Emanuel was the first to expire. Conceived and born into felony, the infant's brief existence was now over. The doughty Emanuel had survived the privations of Botany Bay, the hardships of the boat voyage, the extreme discomforts in the *Rembang*. He was at once the apple of his mother's eye and the symbol of her woe. She concealed the death of his son from her husband, now sunk in vacant-minded lethargy and slipping from her fast. With son, so with father. Life's battle had been too severe, too punishing, the odds too great. The Dutch pastor pronounced the appropriate sentences under the thick foliage of the tropic trees.[1]

Captain Edwards now arranged with the Dutch East India Company for his party to be divided into four parts and to embark them on board four of their ships for Holland at no expense to the British government other than for the officers and prisoners. ('This appeared to me to be the most eligible and least expensive way of getting to England.')

[1] Emanuel Bryant died in Batavia Hospital, 1 December 1791.
William Bryant died in Batavia Hospital, 22 December 1791.

Edwards' Report.

State of the Company of HMS *Pandora*, Captain Edwards, and the manner disposed of on board the Company's ships for their voyage to Europe

Ship *Zwan* Lieut. John Larkan & 17 ratings
    Horssen Lt. Robert Corner, Surgeon Hamilton and 16 others
    Hoornwey Lt. Thos. Hayward & 17 others
    Vreedenberg Mr. G. Passmore, Master
                Mr. G. Bentham, Purser and 20 others
    I embarked in the *Vreedenberg* in which were carried the ten pirates, bound to Amsterdam. Half the convicts on board the *Hoornwey* and half on the *Horssen*.

Whole number of ship's company saved in ship & tender	99[1]
Supernumeraries, viz. Pirates	10
Convicts 4 men, one woman ..	5
	114

Edward Edwards.

A List of Convicts, deserters from Port Jackson, delivered to Captain Edwards of His Majesty's ship *Pandora* by Timotheus Wanjon, Governor of the Dutch settlements at Timor, 5th October 1791

William Allen
John Butcher
Nathaniel Lilley
James Martin
Mary Bryant (transported by the name of Mary Broad)
William Morton
William Bryant (Died Hospital Batavia)
James Cox
John Simms
Emanuel Bryant (Died Hospital Batavia)   } Children of the above
Charlotte Bryant   }   Wm. & Mary Bryant.

                                            Edward Edwards.

It may be necessary to observe that the above convicts have several names and that Wm. Bryant and James Cox pretended that their time of transportation had expired. These two found a boat and money to procure necessaries to enable themselves and others to escape, for which I presume they are liable to punishment and think it my duty to give information.

                                              E.E.

[1] There is a discrepancy in Capt. Edwards' figures; 89 of the ship's company were saved, plus nine from the schooner, making 98 not 99.

In the course of the next few weeks the ships sailed from Batavia homeward bound via the Cape of Good Hope. One of the convicts on board the *Hoornwey*, bound for Rotterdam, was James Cox, transported to Botany Bay for life, having been sentenced at the Exeter Assizes on 24 May 1784. As they passed down through Sunda Strait the prisoners were ordered up on deck for their daily crawl round the hatches. Cox was in the canvas privy, perched precariously in the starboard chains. He gazed at the passing shores; his right ankle showed the red weal of his leg iron; his wasted frame on which his rags hung loosely gave no evidence of strength to reach those inviting beaches. Even if he did gain the uncertain liberty of those tumbling waters below, the ship would be hove to, a boat lowered and his attempted escape be followed by a spell at the triangle. To many, the fear of the cat was the beginning of wisdom. But James Cox was past all fear and all wisdom.

Perhaps at this moment of crisis he remembered the bright if deceitful eyes of Sarah Young. He had been tempted to marry her since they were both lifers, a man might as well have a wife and such marriages were encouraged by the Botany Bay authorities. But then he had caught her in other men's arms, his eyes were opened and he had rid himself of his lustful desires and secretly joined Bryant's escape party. That last night, before the escape, he had got Bryant who could read and write to scribble a note to Sarah, at his dictation: 'Do you give over those vices that I have caught you at more than once, or you will come to a bad end.'

Now he too was come to a bad end.

The next moment he was overboard, with the mad prompting in his brain to reach the shore. The ship swept on, but his fall or dive had been seen. The master of the ship ran to the stern, caught sight of his bobbing head. Instinctively he turned to shout orders, to put the helm down, to launch the boat. . . .

But the English lieutenant, Thomas Hayward, cried out: 'No no! Sail on! He may escape the gallows, but not the sharks!'

The ship sailed on.

The epitaph was written by Captain Edwards: 'James Cox, Dd, fell overboard Straits of Sunda' and by Surgeon Hamilton: 'In our passage from Batavia to the Cape, one of the convicts had jumped overboard in the night and swam to the Dutch arsenal at Honroost.'

But did he?

At the point where Cox jumped overboard, off Thwartway Island, the channel is four miles wide. He would thus have had to swim a maximum distance of two miles to reach either shore. His fate remained unknown, though it was conjectured that he would have been swept out to sea by the strong current in the Strait.

James Cox was not the only one. There was another of the escaped convicts on board the *Hoornwey*, William Morton, no lifer but only a seven-year man. Not that it mattered very much whether the sentence was life, twenty, or seven years. The British government had no intention whatever of allowing time-expired men, or women, ever to return to their native land. Transportation meant 'for life'. William Morton had been sentenced at Maidstone Assizes to seven years in July 1785, and it was now 1792. By the time he reached England he would have been time-expired, but with the crime of escaping hanging over his head.

At any rate, whatever his prospects, William Morton no longer took any interest. His body, shrouded and shotted, lay on a hatch cover on the ship's rail. A few perfunctory words were uttered, two of the men tilted the hatch cover and the body of Morton slid forward and downward into the sea.

'William Morton, Dd. on board Dutch East India Co's ship *Hoornwey*' wrote Captain Edwards.

'We met nothing particular en route,' wrote Surgeon Hamilton, 'but experienced great death and sickness in going through the Straits of Sunda.'

As for Mary Bryant, she began to regain her health and her spirits as the ship moved steadily across the ocean towards the Cape. Life was less terrible in the Indiaman where order, cleanliness and discipline prevailed. With Charlotte playing by her side, she sewed clothes for herself and the child and washed when a bucket of water became available. With the exception of his brief daily inspection, Lieut. Hayward left them alone.

They were allowed to lie on deck unencumbered by irons, for he was indifferent as to whether they jumped overboard – or not. In these more salubrious surroundings pirates and convicts regained health and strength, all except Samuel Bird who had privily changed his name to John Simms. That was the name he had given to Captain Edwards in Coupang and that was the name under which he lay dying in the *Hoornwey*. . . . But to Mary Bryant, as she bent over the dying man, he was Samuel Bird. These two had travelled a long way together and now he was leaving her. At this rate she would soon be the last survivor. He confided to her that he was not Sam Bird at all, but John Simms. He didn't wish to bring convict shame on the family name, but when they got clear away from Botany

Bay he reckoned he was a free man at last, and as a free man went back to his proper name.

That evening they backed the mainyard of the *Hoornwey* once again and John Simms alias Samuel Bird followed Morton into the deep.

'John Simms, Dd. on board Dutch East India's Co's ship *Hoornwey*.'

Three weeks later the *Hoornwey* came to an anchor in Table Bay where the *Horssen* and the *Vreedenburg* had already arrived.

Chapter 27

Aboard the *Gorgon*

AMONG the shipping in Table Bay was HMS *Gorgon* flying British colours, a welcome sight to Captain Edwards and his men. He immediately went on board and found Captain John Parker in command. To his brother officer, Edwards related the story of his trials and sufferings and requested a passage to England for his men, the pirates and the convicts.

Captain Parker had recently arrived from New South Wales and his accommodation was already well filled with officers, Marines and other details from New Holland. He agreed, however, to find space for Captain Edwards' party. They could be accommodated in odd corners in the hold, and as for the pirates and convicts, anything would do for them.

But what of the woman convict with a child of five? Captain Parker himself was a married man, and the apple of his eye was a small daughter aged five. What was more to the point was that Mrs Parker was on board the *Gorgon*, captains in those days being allowed greater liberty in the matter of wives at sea. When he had asked her if she would like to go with him on a voyage round the world, she had eagerly assented. There was an interesting outcome of Mary Ann Parker's voyage. Shortly after the *Gorgon* reached England, her husband died, leaving her with a young daughter, a posthumous son and inadequate means. With her left arm supporting her infant son and her right hand holding the pen, she proceeded to write a book:

A Voyage Round the World in H.M.S. Gorgon, Captain John Parker. Performed and written by his widow for the advantage of a numerous family. [London, 1795.]

The numerous family consisted of the said two children which in those days, when families of a round dozen were normal, would not have been considered 'numerous'.

Another thing about Mary Ann was that she seems to have been greatly taken with Captain Edwards. This hard-faced bully, this cruel scoundrel whom nearly every writer since has condemned in harshest terms seems to her to have been an agreeable and amiable character whose company was extremely pleasant on the long passage home.

Mary Ann Parker writes:

On the 18th March a Dutch Indiaman arrived from Batavia, and shortly afterward we were gratified with the company of Captain Edwards of his Majesty's ship *Pandora*. A few days after landing, he embarked and pursued his voyage in our ship.

The convicts also who had escaped from Port Jackson were taken up by the *Pandora* at Coupang and were returned to England in the *Gorgon*.

The *Gorgon* had brought from New Holland no fewer than 109 officers, non-commissioned officers and privates together with twenty-five wives and forty-seven children of the New South Wales Corps.[1] To these were now added Captain Edwards' ship's company, the pirates and the convicts.

Brief entries in the log of the *Gorgon* supply the details.

Sunday March 18 1792. Moored in Table Bay. Anchored here a Dutch Indiaman from Batavia, with Captain Edwards of His Majesty's ship *Pandora* and sundry of his ship's company in her. . . .

Tuesday, March 20 . . . Came on board from the Dutch ship 10 pirates belong to His Majesty's ship *Bounty*, brought here by Captain Edwards.

Friday, March 23 . . . Recd. from the Dutch ship William Allen, Mary Bryant and Charlotte Bryant, supposed convicts deserted from Port Jackson.

Monday, April 2 . . . Came on board three convicts supposed to have deserted from Port Jackson – John Butcher, Nath'l Lilley, James Martin. . . .

Tuesday, April 3 . . . Came on board Captain Edwards of His Maj's late ship *Pandora* for passage to England.

Friday, April 6 . . . Sailed for England.

And Mrs Mary Ann Parker noted in her Journal: 'Our bark was also crowded with Kangaroos, Opossums and every curiosity which that country produced. The Quarter deck was occupied with shrubs and plants.'

The 'bark', really a frigate, was also crowded with all the stores and equipment salved from HMS *Guardian* which had been wrecked on an iceberg and was magnificently saved and sailed back to Table Bay by the

---

[1] This was the New South Wales Corps which garrisoned the convict colony at a time when England was fighting Napoleon. Its officers and men engaged in the sale of imported liquor, the so-called rum traffic, the chief blot on the colony. 'Rum flowed like water and was drunk like wine.' The regiment was labelled by the ribald community the Rum Puncheon Corps. The arrest of Governor Bligh, who had attempted to suppress the traffic, was known as the Rum Rebellion.

celebrated Captain Riou. Her anchors were left by Captain Parker 'in case a passing ship might require one'.

According to Morrison, life on board the *Gorgon* for the ten pirates was a very pleasant change. They were now treated humanely for the first time since their arrest. They were placed on the regulation two-thirds allowance for rations, etc., which, says Morrison:

Was now thought feasting. McIntosh, Coleman and Norman were at liberty, and the rest of us only one leg in irons and every indulgence given and Lieut. Gardner of this ship, in the absence of Capt. Parker, very humanely gave us a sail to lay on which by us was thought a luxury; and was indeed such as we had not enjoy'd for 12 months before.

The convicts, too, were much better situated in the *Gorgon*. To the passengers and crew of the *Gorgon*, the story of their escape from Botany Bay was well known, and was passed from person to person in a confused jumble in which the mutiny in the *Bounty*, the wreck of the *Pandora* and the capture of the escaped convicts was all mixed up. It was exciting, not to say sensational, and here among them were the pirates and the convicts, in person. Including the woman! And her child.

The story of her escape in the open boat with an infant in arms was the topic of the day. It was said that she had originated and led the escapade; that she was dressed in men's clothing; that she was captain of the boat's crew; that she had suckled the infant in the boat; that her husband or paramour had failed to rise to her level of endurance, and that she had successfully hoodwinked the Dutch authorities in Coupang.

It was whispered among the soldiers' wives that she was not a woman at all but a youth who, for his own purposes, had assumed female disguise. Some opined that she was a hussy, no better than a common prostitute. The senior lady on board, wife of the major of the NSW Corps, let it be known that she was not a fit subject for the compassion and condescension of the ladies of the regiment, which was pretty rich coming from the Rum Corps.[1]

As for Mary Ann Parker, she was not interested in such a low creature, and made no mention of her in her book.

But the sentiment and the sentimentality of the men of the *Gorgon*, of

[1] In this depraved and licentious community, drunkenness was rife, concubines were included in official returns, illegitimate children exceeded in number the legitimate, prostitutes accompanied officers in their carriages to the parade ground while wives remained neglected at home, everybody was defrauding the Government, profiteering was rampant and secret stills were in every other house.

Rawson, *Bligh of the* Bounty.

the *Pandora* and of the NSW Corps were evoked by the spectacle of this Cornish heroine and her fatherless child.

As was also that of Captain Watkin Tench. No Rum Corps man he, but a genuine Marine.

Captain Tench had been the officer in command of the guards in the transport *Charlotte* in which ship Mary Bryant's baby Charlotte was born. He was a passenger in the *Gorgon* and was particularly interested in Mary Bryant. He writes:

She told me that they coasted the shores of New Holland, putting occasionally into different harbours which they found in going along. Here they hauled their bark ashore, payed her seams with tallow and repaired her. But it was not without difficulty they could keep off the attacks of the Indians. These people harassed them so much that they quitted the mainland. Between the latitudes of 26 and 27 south, they found plenty of large turtles. Soon after they closed again with the Continent, when the boat got entangled in the surf, was driven on shore and they had all well-nigh perished. They passed through the Straits of Endeavour, and beyond the Gulf of Carpentaria they found a large freshwater river which they entered and filled their empty casks. Until they reached the Gulf of Carpentaria, they saw no natives or canoes differing from those about Port Jackson. But now they were chased by large canoes, fitted with sails and fighting stages, and capable of holding thirteen each. They had escaped by dint of rowing to windward.

On 5 June, 1791 they reached Timor. . . .

I confess that I never looked at these people without pity and astonishment. They had miscarried in a heroic struggle for liberty after having combated every hardship and conquered every difficulty.

The woman and one of the men[1] had gone out to Botany Bay in the same ship which took me thither (*Charlotte*). They had both been distinguished for good behaviour and I could not but reflect with admiration the strange combination of circumstances which had again brought us together, to baffle human foresight and to confound human speculation.[2]

[1] James Martin, author of the *Memorandoms* (see Appendix B).
[2] Tench, *Account of the Settlement at Port Jackson.*

Chapter 28

Fate of the Convicts

THE *Gorgon* had sailed from Table Bay on 6 April and St Helena was sighted on 18 April. As the ship ran into a colder clime, the child Charlotte sickened, and on 6 May the officer of the watch noted down the routine entries in the log book, after which he added:

'Sunday, May 6 . . . a.m. at 6, departed this life Charlotte Bryant, daughter of Mary Bryant, convict.'

Since the child was not borne on the strength of His Majesty's naval or military forces, and her name was not included on the Register of Ration Issues, her existence was unofficial. It was irregular, improper and she fitted into no known category. The child of convict joy had voyaged to the antipodes, sailed in a boat to the distant Timor, journeyed to the Cape and sailed homeward bound up the broad Atlantic.

Born at sea, she died at sea, after four and a half years of ceaseless wandering. Nothing remained but to bury her. The chaplain made discreet enquiries. Though Mary Bryant had no marriage lines to produce, she was the lawfully wedded wife of the late William Bryant, as Captain Watkin Tench could testify. It appeared also that the child had been baptized in the *Charlotte* as Captain Tench could also witness. He remembered the occasion well because:

about this time, some female convicts on board different ships increased the number of souls on board by an addition of seven children . . . the christenings were kept on board the respective ships with great glee, and an additional allowance being distributed to the crews of these ships where births took place . . .[1]

Thus satisfied, the chaplain agreed to officiate with due formality: 'It hath pleased Thee to deliver this, our sister out of the miseries of this sinful world. . . .'

The words seemed to have a peculiar application to the child who had witnessed so much of this sinful world, but any such reflections were disturbed and dissipated. As Charlotte slipped into the deep, there came

[1] Historical Records, NSW, vol. II, p. 740.

the harsh cry: 'Square the main yard!' The watch on deck ran to the braces, as the bo'sun's mates shrilled their pipes and the flag, temporarily half-masted, was hoisted again.

It seemed to be the *Gorgon*'s requiem for the little girl.

That evening the officer made a further entry in the log book.

'Monday, May 7 . . . p.m. at 4 committed the body of the deceased to the deep.'

Some evenings later there was a stir on deck and noises and shouts were heard. The woman convict learned that the Lizard light was in view. Here was her native land, Cornwall. There lay Falmouth, St Just, Dodman Point and Fowey. After more than five years she had returned. No hand waved farewell to her then: no welcome home could she expect now as the *Gorgon* beat up Channel to Spithead where she came to anchor.

It was 20 June 1792. The long trek was over, over for the troops and Marines, for Captain Edwards and his men, for the pirates and the convicts, and for Mrs Mary Ann Parker.

Her voyage was ended, too. Her husband was busily engaged and she was delighted to accept the proffered escort of Captain Edwards to the shore.

He accompanied me on shore and after four hours rowing against wind and tide we landed at the Sally Port at Portsmouth. I had the happiness of embracing a little daughter who is at this present time one of my greatest comforts, my other child, a boy, having died in my absence.

And here we take leave of Mrs Parker, and of Captain Edwards, also. He was honourably acquitted by the Court for the loss of his ship and continued to serve in the navy. In 1799 he became a rear-admiral and died in 1815, the year of Waterloo, aged seventy-three.

The *Bounty* mutineers were removed to HMS *Hector*, there to await their trial and Captain Parker notified the Admiralty that he had five convicts on board under arrest. A few days later the Bow Street magistrates sent for the prisoners and they were rowed on shore and taken up to Newgate.

NEWGATE. JULY SESSIONS 1792[1]

1792	Entry No.	Names	Crime
5 July	93	Will Allen	Transports found
		Jno. Butcher	at large before
		Nat. Lilley	the expiration of
		Jas. Martin	sentence
		Mary Bryant	Committed to
		alias Broad	Newgate

[1] P.R.O., H.O. 26/1 Newgate Register.

As for Nat. Lilley and Will Allen, being 'lifers' they were duly returned to Botany Bay to complete their sentences and to fade into the obscurity that attended lifers.

John Butcher was permitted to enlist in the Rum Corps and sailed for the colony once again. Mary Bryant's old friend James Martin disappears also, leaving a strange echo behind him. (See Appendix B.)

As for Mary Bryant, she had been originally sentenced to death,[1] she had been reprieved, she had been transported to Botany Bay, she had escaped, been rearrested and now lay in Newgate as a 'convict at large'. She had lost her husband, her two children, her liberty – and her youth.

What was to become of her?

Sir Basil Thomson stated categorically that: 'the woman survived to obtain a full pardon, owing chiefly to the exertions of an [unnamed] officer of marines who went home with her in the *Gorgon*, and eventually married her', but he gave no authority for this statement.

The truth was not revealed until the publication in 1934 of Volume XVIII of *The Private Papers of James Boswell* by Professor F. A. Pottle of Yale University, and his subsequent volume *The Girl from Botany Bay*.[2]

At this nadir of her fortunes, Mary Bryant and the four men convicts in Newgate found a powerful and interested friend in James Boswell himself.

Early in 1792 he read about them in the newspapers, went to Newgate to interview them, and being impressed with their miserable condition applied himself to gaining a pardon for them in which he succeeded in the case of the woman.

MARY BRYANT (ALIAS BROAD)

WHEREAS Mary Bryant alias Broad stands charged with escaping before the expiration of the term for which she had been ordered to be transported and
WHEREAS some favourable circumstances have been humbly presented unto us on her behalf, inducing us to extend our grace and mercy unto her and to grant her our free pardon for her said crime
OUR WILL AND PLEASURE is that you cause the said Mary Bryant (alias

---

[1] Sir Basil Thomson, Owen Rutter, Dr Mackaness and other authorities all state that Mary Bryant was convicted for 'connivance in her lover's escape from gaol'.
The charge sheet gives a different version:
'For feloniously assaulting Agnes Lakeman Sptr. in the King's highway, feloniously putting her in corporal fear of her life, and feloniously and violently taking from her person in the said highway one silk Bonnet val. 12d. and other goods val. £1. 11s. her property.' Mary Broad was charged with three other girls, Catherine Fryer, Mary Haydon and Mary Shepherd of assaulting and robbing the spinster. Presumably they were village hoydens. Technically this was highway robbery with violence, and all four girls were sentenced to be hanged.
[2] Viking Press, New York, 1937.

Broad) to be forthwith discharged out of custody and that she be incerted for her said crime in our first and next general pardon that shall come out for the poor convicts in Newgate without any condition whatsoever . . .

By His Majesty's Command

2nd May 1793   HENRY DUNDAS

Boswell provided her with funds for her support, paid the passage money for her to go to Fowey in the schooner *Anne and Elizabeth* and promised her an annuity of £10 per annum. She could not write so he arranged for her to sign 'M.B.' as receipts for the half-yearly payments. All this seems to have been done out of a spirit of sheer philanthropy by Boswell and there is no evidence that he was moved by any other consideration.

There is no further record of Mary Bryant, of her remarriage or of anything else about her. A Mary Bryant is registered in the Fowey Parish Register as being married in 1807, fifteen years after her return to Fowey when she would be forty-two. This may have been the ex-convict, but Professor Pottle thinks not. He concluded his account of her story, as revealed by Boswell's Papers: 'I know of no one whom I should more proudly claim as my forbear than that heroic girl who escaped from Botany Bay and was befriended by James Boswell.'

Chapter 29

Fate of the Pirates

THE utter insignificance of the *Bounty–Pandora* affair becomes evident when seen against the immense historical background at the time. While the news of the mutiny was intriguing England, Washington was named first President. The Bastille fell. While Captain Bligh was publishing his *Narrative of the Mutiny*, Burke was publishing his *Reflections*; while Captain Edwards was scouring the Pacific in the *Pandora*, Boulton and Watt were finding the first customers for their Improved Steam Engine, and Wilberforce was urging the House of Commons to abolish the slave trade.

On the very day that the court martial assembled for the trial of the *Bounty* mutineers, the heads of the first victims rolled from the guillotine.[1]

The trial or rather court martial of the mutineers from the *Bounty* opened in HMS *Duke* at Portsmouth on 12 September 1792, three months after their return. No fewer than twelve captains were assembled under Admiral Lord Hood to hear the case, which continued until 18 September.

The Court found the charges not proved against Charles Norman, Josiah Coleman, Thos. McIntosh, and Michael Byrne, and acquitted them.

The Court found that the charges had been proved against Peter Heywood, James Morrison, Thomas Ellison, Thomas Burkitt, John Millward and William Muspratt, and adjudged them to suffer death by being hanged by the neck.

But the Court, in consideration of various circumstances, did humbly and most earnestly recommend the said Peter Heywood and James Morrison to his Majesty's Royal Mercy.

The Court's 'most earnest recommendation to mercy' was of course tantamount to a full and free pardon, and Heywood and Morrison were in due course released.

---

[1] 'For lo, the great Guillotine, wondrous to behold, now stands there; the Doctor's *Idea* has become oak and iron; the huge cyclopean axe falls in its grooves like the ram of the pile engine, swiftly snuffing out the lives of men.' Carlyle.

Muspratt was defended by a skilful lawyer, Stephen Barney. Although Muspratt had been unable to convince the Court of his innocence, he escaped by the skin of his teeth on a technical point of law raised by the astute lawyer and was subsequently freed.

The final tally of the fourteen mutineers was therefore as follows:

Josiah Coleman Michael Byrne Charles Norman Thos. McIntosh	} Acquitted
P. Heywood J. Morrison	} Pardoned after being convicted
Geo. Stewart R. Skinner H. Hillbrant J. Sumner	} Drowned in *Pandora*
W. Muspratt	Reprieved after being convicted[1]
Thos. Burkitt J. Millward Thos. Ellison	} Hanged

During the trial, public interest was centred upon Peter Heywood largely on account of his youth and influential connections, and also because of the frantic efforts of his elder sister Nessy to secure his acquittal. She constituted herself his chief advocate and defender. She and her mother were prepared to mortgage everything they possessed, and to spare no expense in securing the best possible counsel. They were informed, however, that naval Courts were unimpressed by the rhetoric of civilian counsel.

'We don't like sea lawyers, or land lawyers either,' wrote their uncle, Commodore Pasley, who instead secured the good offices of a former Judge Advocate with long experience of naval Courts.

Among the immense number of letters written by Nessy on her brother's behalf was one to Lord Chatham, First Lord.

My Lord . . . When I assure you that he is dearer and more precious to me than any object on earth—nay, infinitely more valuable than Life itself . . . that upon his fate my own and (shall I not add?) that of a tender, fond and alas! widowed mother depends . . .

[1] Sir Basil Thomson in a footnote shows Muspratt as being hanged. In fact, he was reprieved.

But Lord Chatham made no response.

When not writing letters, Nessy composed poems to ease her anguish.

ANXIETY

Doubting dreading fretful guest
Quit, oh! quit this mortal breast
Why wilt thou my peace invade
And each brighter prospect shade?
Pain me not with needless Fear
But let Hope my bosom cheer.

In a letter during the course of the trial which she followed with agonized concern, Nessy wrote:

With respect to that little wretch Hallett, his intrepidity in Court was astonishing. After everyone had spoken so highly in Peter's favour and testified so strongly to his innocence that not a doubt was entertained of his acquittal, Hallett declared *unasked* that Peter, on hearing what Mr. Bligh said to him, *laughed* and turned contemptuously away.

No other witness saw Peter laugh but Hallett. On the contrary, all agreed he wore a countenance remarkably sorrowful, yet the effect of this *cruel* evidence was wonderful upon the minds of the Court.

So much for 'that little wretch Hallett' whose evidence, by the way, placed James Morrison also in the gravest danger of being hanged. Hallett stated that Morrison leaned over the taffrail and called down to Captain Bligh and his people in the boat: 'If my friends at home enquire after me, tell them I'm somewhere in the South Seas!'

Hallett said that Morrison called this out in a jeering manner, the effect of which, in Nessy's phrase, was 'wonderful upon the minds of the Court'.

On receiving the long-hoped-for news that her brother had been pardoned, Nessy, who had worn herself out in her efforts to secure his release, wrote to her mother in the Isle of Man:

London. 26 October 4 o'clock.

Oh blessed hour! Little did I think when I closed my letter this morning that before night I should be out of my senses with joy – this moment, this ecstatic moment brought the news that the Pardon is on its way to Portsmouth!

In a few hours our Angel will be free!

Tomorrow, next day at farthest I shall be. . . .

Oh Heavens! what shall I be? I am already transported, even to Pain. Then how shall I bear to clasp him to the bosom of your happy, oh how happy

Nessy.

At last Peter was freed.

> 29 October. half past ten o'clock – the
> brightest moment of my existence!
>
> My dearest Mamma, I have seen him, clasped him to my bosom and my felicity
> is beyond expression. In person he is even now as I could wish; in mind you know
> him to be an Angel.
>
> The three happiest beings at this moment on earth are your most dutiful and
> affectionate children
>
> NESSY HEYWOOD
> PETER HEYWOOD
> JANE HEYWOOD.

Nessy however was not long permitted to enjoy her new-found felicity.
Within a few months of her brother's liberation, she died of consumption,
or as it is now termed, tuberculosis.

Midshipman Peter Heywood now leaves the scene to re-enter the
Service in which he rose eventually to the rank of captain. The normal
routine of his naval life was interrupted astonishingly sixteen years after
the court martial by a strange incident narrated by Sir John Barrow in his
Eventful History.

About the year 1808 and 1809, a very general opinion was prevalent in Cumberland and Westmoreland that Christian was there and made frequent private visits
to an aunt living there. Christian was well known in the district but this might be
passed over as mere gossip, had not a singular circumstance happened about the
same time, for the truth of which the Editor [Barrow] does not hesitate to vouch.

In Fore Street, Plymouth Dock, Captain Heywood found himself walking
behind a man whose shape had so much the appearance of Christian's, that he
involuntarily quickened his pace.

Both were walking very fast, and the rapid steps behind him having aroused
the stranger's attention, he suddenly turned his face, looked at Heywood, and
immediately ran off.

But the face was as much like Christian's as the back. Heywood, exceedingly
excited, ran also. Both ran as fast as they were able but the stranger had the advantage and upon making several short turns, disappeared. . . .

Heywood's first thought was to set about making further enquiries but on
recollection of the pain and trouble such a discovery must occasion, he considered
it more prudent to let the matter drop. . . .

Perhaps Sir John Barrow vouched for the truth of this yarn because
Heywood confided it to him as a high Admiralty official to whom it was
Heywood's duty to report it. It was not for either the captain or the
Secretary to condone and even conceal the escape of a notorious mutineer.

But by now the mutiny was long since forgotten. If it were indeed Christian, his arrest and trial would reopen old wounds. Sixteen years had passed . . . better let sleeping dogs lie. So the Secretary advised, if he did not order the captain to remain silent. Christian vanished, not for the first time. . . .

And Captain Peter Heywood also, back into the Silent Service.

Last but not least there lingers upon the scene that strange voluble creature – James Morrison. No dour Scot he, but a bright, effusive wordy fellow, watchful, observant, recording, always setting it down. Here is a man who has seen Death at close hand several times, and evaded or avoided him, somehow.

Drowning, shooting, hanging, he had escaped each time.

Here, too, is the prime author of the *Bounty–Pandora* story. He has seen it all, been through it all, from the day the *Bounty* sailed on *her* last voyage to the *Pandora*'s last voyage, to the court martial, to freedom. Here, too, is the skilled naval architect who designed a first-class schooner that later sailed around the world. And here is a mere petty officer who was anything but petty in his nature. For example, he was loyal to his Captain Bligh: 'The behaviour of his officers on this occasion was dastardly beyond description. The least attempt by them to rescue the ship would have been effected had an attempt been made . . .' and Morrison had no love for Bligh.

And he was just to his Captain Edwards: when the Dutch Indiaman *Rembang* was conveying the *Pandora* party from Coupang to Batavia, she was struck by a cyclone and in grave danger. Morrison recorded years later: This ship [*Rembang*] was badly found and worse managed, and if Captain Edwards had not taken the command and set his men to work, she would never have reached Batavia.'

No petty mind, that.

Morrison seems to have had some curious quirks in his nature. Why, for example, should this would-be reformer, this critic of the Establishment, when to be a radical was regarded as being worse than a Communist today, why should he have chosen the Most Noble Order of the Garter for his tattoo-pattern when he was 'pricked' on Tahiti? 'Tattooed with a Star under his left breast and a garter round his left leg with the motto *Honi soit qui mal y pense.*'

During his stay at Tahiti he became the *Tayo* and equal of the reigning chieftain over whom he exercised great influence and the reigning chieftain Matte or Tinah or Otoo was on the way to becoming King Pomare the First, Sovereign of all Tahiti.

One would have thought that by now, after all he had gone through and his criticisms of authority, the man would have become disenchanted with the sea life, and with the stern discipline of the navy. He had joined the Service in 1779 at the age of seventeen and knew no other trade. Now in 1793, having completed his Journal, he was thirty-three years of age and unemployed. In this situation, he applied to rejoin the navy. With the Napoleonic wars looming, there were plenty of vacancies for skilled men in a Service which was largely manned by pressed men.

Petty Officer James Morrison, in his humble station, now passes into obscurity, serving his king and country like thousands of other seamen through the heroic period of St Vincent, the Nile, Copenhagen and Trafalgar.

His last ship was the *Blenheim*, flagship of Admiral Sir Thomas Trou-bridge on the East Indies station, based on Penang. The Admiral was ordered to the Cape to take up the command on that station, but the *Blenheim* was in no condition to sail. She was in a bad state and quite unseaworthy but the Admiral was impatient to reach his new station. The *Blenheim* was escorted by HMS *Harrier* which was commanded by Captain Troubridge, the Admiral's son. They sailed from Penang in December 1806, bound for the Cape via Madras. On 1 February 1807, in a frightful gale off the Madagascar coast the old ship foundered, with all hands.

Among them was James Morrison, Gunner RN.

So ends:

> As true a tale of dangers past
> As ever the dark annals of the deep
> Disclosed for man to dread
> Or woman weep.

Appendix A

THE first full length account of the mutiny in the *Bounty*, excluding Bligh's own *Narrative*, was published many years later by no less a personage than the Second Secretary to the Admiralty, Sir John Barrow. This gentleman, while occupying this high position at the Admiralty, published his own *Eventful History of the Mutiny*, a highly partisan account which blamed Captain Bligh and condoned the mutiny, though not actually approving it, probably too much even for a high Admiralty official to countenance.

He published his book anonymously at first, and it became very popular and has remained the classic account of the mutiny. Like Southey's *Life of Nelson*, it survives to this day, though far better volumes on the subjects have been given to the world by later writers. There was a difference in the approach of the authors to their subject. Barrow disliked Bligh; Southey adored Nelson.

It might indeed seem a little improper for Sir John Barrow, while still in office, to give to the public his own account, heavily biased as it was, of a highly controversial subject. It may be that Barrow's book first spread the story and painted the picture of Bligh, 'the bully and the brute', that prevailed throughout the nineteenth century and was not finally dispelled until recent times, notably by Dr George Mackaness in his *Life of Vice-Admiral Bligh*, which gives the facts rather than the fictions.

Appendix B

AT SOME time Bligh was shown Morrison's *Journal*, and indignantly refuted the charges made against him by Morrison. His angry phrases include: the villainy of this Morrison; these low charges strongly mark the character of Morrison; this Morrison was the worst of the mutineers next to Christian and Churchill, if not their adviser.

When Morrison notes that symptoms of scurvy appeared in the *Bounty*, Bligh retorts: Captain Bligh never had a symptom of the scurvy in any ship he commanded.

Bligh sharply answered fourteen specific charges against himself in Morrison's *Journal* and concluded: 'Among all these charges there is not one of cruelty or oppression.' Complaints about rations and such-like did not worry Bligh so much as the growing volume of criticism that he was a cruel tyrant and a bully. He therefore seized upon the omission of charges on this score and specifically referred to this omission because these accusations were those that 'wounded him most'.

Appendix C

In 1937, Mr Charles Blount of Pembroke College, Cambridge, was working on the Jeremy Bentham papers in University College, London. By chance he came upon a rough folder containing twenty-three sheets of paper, written on one side only, entitled:

Memorandoms by James Martin

James Martin was one of the convicts sent out to Botany Bay in the transport *Charlotte*, the same vessel in which Mary Bryant sailed. He was closely associated with her from the time they were embarked in the *Charlotte* for the passage to New Holland until their return, still in company, to Newgate five years later.

Mr Blount states:

When James Martyn (or Martin) was committed to Newgate, he collected what paper he could in the prison, and commenced to write an account of his journey. But he was illiterate and after a time he grew tired and dictated the remainder of his story to three of his fellow prisoners – of varying degrees of illiteracy. Since only four of the original eight convicts survived the journey back to England, it is pleasant to think that the four handwritings in which the Memorandoms is recorded represent the hands of James Martyn, William Allen, James Brown[1] and Nathaniel Lilley. (See page 36.)

MEMORANDOMS BY JAMES MARTIN

I James Martin Being Convicted at they City of Exeter in they County of Devonshire Being found guilty of Stealing 16½ lb of old Lead and 4½ lb of old Iron property of Lord Courney[2] powdrum cacle[3] nere Exeter. Recevd sentance for to be Transported to Botany Bay for 7 years – Returned from thy Bar to Exeter goal and there remaind 2 months – from thence sent on Board they Dunkirk there remaind 10 months from thence put on board they *Charlotte* Transport Then Bound to Botany Bay – March 12 1787 Saild round to Spithead there remaind tothey 13 of May – then sail in Copany with 10 sail for Botany Bay under Commandand of govoner Philips.

Made they Peek of Tenereef 5 Day of June, there remaind 7 days, then saild for

---

[1] alias John Butcher.   [2] Courtenay.   [3] Powderham Castle, near Exeter.

they Island of Reiodeginera,[1] being 8 weks on our passage – there remain one Month then saild for they Cape of good hope – being Eight weeks and three Days on our passage – then Saild for Botany Bay Being 10 weeks on our passage – Came to an anchor in Port Jackson Send on Shore in two Days – they Convicts Being Sent on Shore So Began to work on governments account on being landed we were Encamped and fourmed in sqads of six in a tent – after we Bing Encamped We Some were sent to Clear they ground Others sent to Build huts—

I remaind on the Island from January, 1788 unto March 1791 – on the 28 Day of March Made My Escape in Compy with 7 men more and me with one woman and two Childn – in an open six oar Boat – having of provision on Bd one hundred wt of flower and one hundd st of Rice 14 lb of pork and aBout Eight galons of water – having a Copass Quardrant and Chart. after two Days sail reach a little Creek aBout 2 Degrees to they Northward of port Jackson there found a quantity of fine Burng Coal there Remaind 2 nights and one Day and found aVarse[2] Quantty of Cabage tree which we cut Down and procured they Cabage.

Then they Natives Came Down to which we gave some Cloathes and other articles and they went away very much satisfied.

They appearance of they land appears more better here than at Sidney Cove[3] here we got avarse Quantity of fish which of a great Refresment to us – After our stay of 2 nights and one Day we proceeded our Voyage to they Northward after 2 Days sail we made a very fine harbour Seeming to run up they Country for Many miles and Quite Comodious for they Anchorage of Shipping – here we found aplenty of fresh water – hawld our Boat ashore to repair her Bottom being very leaky they Better to pay her Bottom with some Beeswax and Rosin which we had a small Quantity Thereof – But on they Same night was Drove of By they natives – which meant to destroy us – we Launchd our Boat and Road off in they strame Quite out of Reach of them – that being Sunday Monday we were of in ye stream we rowed Lower Down thinging to Land Some Miles Below – on Monday Morng we Attempted to land when we found a place Convenient for to Repair our Boat we accordg we put some of our things – part being ashore there Came they natives in Vase Numbers With Speers and Sheilds etc. we formed in parts one party of us Made towards them they Better By signes to pasify them But they not taking they least notice accordingly we fired a musket thinking to afright them But they took not they least notice Thereof – on perceving Them Rush more forward we were forsed to take to our Boat and to get out of their reach as fast as we Could – and what to Do we Could not tell But on Consulting with each other it was Detirmined for to row up they harbour which accordingly we rowed up they harbour 9 or 10 miles till we made a little white Sandy Isld in they Middle of they harbour – which landd upon and hawld up our Boat and repair her Bottom with what Little materials we had. whilst our Stay of 2 Days we

---

[1] Rio de Janeiro; the convoy crossed the Atlantic to take advantage of the prevailing winds.

[2] a vast.

[3] Sidney Cove—the actual inlet in Port Jackson upon which the colony was established; now Sydney.

had no Interupon[1] from they Natives – then we rowed of to they main where we took in fresh water and a few cabage trees – and then put out to sea – they natives here is quiet naked of a Copper Colour – shock hair – they have Cannoos made of bark then we proceedd they Northard, having a leadg Breez from they S.W. – But that night they wind Changed and Drove us Quite out of sight of Land – which we hawld our having a set of Sails in they Boat accordingly they next Day we Made Close into they land But they Surf rung so very hard we Cd not attempt to land but kept along shore but Making no harbour or Creek for nere three weeks we were much Distressd for water and wood – accordingly perceving they Surf to abate Two of our men swam on shore thinking to get some water But being afraid of they natives which they see in numbers they returnd without any, But a little wood which threw into they water which we took up We put over on the other side of the Bay expecting to meet with a Convenient Harbour we found a little River which with great difficulty we got up our Boat being very leaky at that Time that it was with great difficulty we Could keep her above Water – were we Landed and hawled her up putting some soap in the Seams which Answered very well – at this Place we Cou'd get no Shell Fish or Fish of any kind in this Bay here we stopped two days and two Nights – then we left this Place and went down the Bay about 20 Miles expecting to meet with a Harbor to get some refreshment – but cou'd see none nor the End of the Bay the Wind being favourable we Tack'd about and put to sea the Land here seem'd to be much the same as at Botany Bay – accordingly we up grapling so stood to they Northward but our Boat being very Deep we were obliged to trow all our Cloathing over Board they Better to lighten our Boat as they Sea Breaking over us Quite rapid – that Night we ran into an open Bay and Could see no Place to land at the Surf running that we were Afraid of Staving our Boat to pieces – We came to a Grapling in that Bay the same Night about 2 oClock in the Morng our Grapling Broke and we were drove in the Middle of the Surf Expecting every Moment that our Boat wou'd be Staved to Pieces and every Soul Perish but as God wou'd have we Got our Boat save on Shore without any Loss or damage excepting one Oar we Hauld our Boat up and there remaind two days and 2 Nights there we kindled a Fire with great difficulty everything that we had being very Wet – we Got Plenty of Shell Fish there and Fresh Water the Natives Came down in great Numbers we discharged a Musquet over their Heads and they dispersed immediately and we saw no more of them we put our things in the Boat and with great difficulty we Got out to Sea for 2 or 3 days we had very Bad Weather our Boat Shipping many heavy Seas, so that One Man was always Employed in Bailing out the Water to keep her up – the next Place we made was White Bay being in Lattd 27d 00 we ran down that Bay 2 or 3 leagues before we cou'd see a convenient Place to Land the Surf running very High we saw two Women and 2 Children with a Fire Brand in their Hands at this Place we Landed the two Women being Frightened ran away but we made Signs that we wanted a Light which they Gave us Crying at the same Time in their Way we took our things out of the Boat and put them in two Huts which was

[1] Interruption.

there – the next Morng about 11 oClock a great Number of the Natives Came towards us – as soon as we saw we went to meet them and Fired a Musquet over their Heads as soon as they Heard the report they ran into the Woods and we saw no more of them the Natives there is Quite Naked – there we Stopped two days and two nights; the Surf running so very High that we were in great danger of Staving ye Boat that Night we were drove out to Sea by a heavy Gale of Wind and Current, expecting every Moment to go to the Bottom next Morng saw no Land the Sea running Mountains high we were Under a Close reeft Mainsail and kept so untill Night and then came too under a droge[1] all the Night with her Head to the Sea thinking every Moment to be the last the sea Coming in so heavy upon us every now and then that two hands was Obliged to keep Bailing out and it rained very hard all that Night the next Morng we took our droge in but Could see no Land but Hawling towards the Land to make it as soon as possible the Gale of Wind still Continuing we kept on under a Close reeft Mainsail but cou'd make no Land all that day – I will Leave you to Consider what distress we must be in the Woman and the two little Babies was in a bad Condition everything being so Wet that we Cou'd by no Means light a Fire we had nothing to Eat except a little raw rice at Night we Came too under a droge as we did the Night before the next Morng we took in our droge and kept to the Northwd on purpose to make the Land about 8 oClock we made Land which proved to be a little Island about 30 Leagues from the Main the Surf running so very high we were rather fearful of going in for fear of Staving our Boat but we Concluded amongst Ourselves that we might as well Venture in there as to keep out to Sea that we shou'd every Soul Perish – All round this Island there was nothing but reefs but a little sandy Beach which we got in safe without much damage and haul'd our Boat up out of the way of the Surf we got all our things out of the Boat then we Went to get a Fire which with great difficulty we got a Fire which being almost Starving we put on a little rice for to Cook when we went to this Island we had but one Gallon of fresh Water for there was not a drop of fresh Water to be had on this Island the Island was about one Mile in Circumference after the Tide fell we went to Look for some Shell Fish but found a great Quantity of very fine Large Turtles which was left upon the reef which we turned five of them and hawled them upon the Beach this reef runs about a Mile and half out in the Sea and Intirely dry when low Water we took and killed One of the Turtles and had a noble Meal this Night it rain'd very Hard when we spread our Mainsail and filled our two Breakers full of Water – We staid on this Island six days during that Time we killed twelve Turtles and some of it we Took and dry'd over the fire to take to sea with us. It seemed to us that there had never been any Natives on this Island there is a kind of Fruit grows like unto a Bellpepper which seemed to Taste very well there was a great Quantity of Fowls which stayed at Night in Holes in the ground we Could not think of taking any live Turtles with us because our Boat wou'd not admit of it we Paid the Seams of our Boat all over with Soap before we put to sea at 8 oClock in the Morng and Steered to the Northward; this Island was in Lat. 26d 27m we made the

[1] A sea anchor.

main Land in the Evening we passed a great Number of Small Islands which we put into a great many of them expecting to find some Turtle but never found any in any of the Islands we put into Afterwards we found a great Quantity of Shell Fish but none of them very fit to Eat but being very Hungred we were Glad to eat them and Thank God for it if it had not been for the Shell Fish and the little Turtle that we had we must have Starved very seldom put into any Place but found plenty of Fresh Water but nothing We could find fit to Eat when we Came to the Gulf of Carpentara[1] which is in Latt. 10d 11m we ran down the Gulf Nine or Ten Miles we saw several small Islands on which we saw several of the Natives in two Canoes landing on One of the small Islands we steered down towards them as soon as they saw us they sent their two Canoes round to the Back of the Island with one Man in each of them when we Came down to them they seemed to stand in a posture of defence against us we fired a Musquet over them and immediately they began Firing their Bows and Arrows at us we immediately hoisted up our Sails and rowed away from them but as God wou'd have it none of their Arrows Came into the Boat but dropped along side we Could not get Hold of any of them but they seemed to be about Eighteen Inches long the Natives seemed to be very Stout and fat and Blacker they were in other Parts we seen before there was One which we took to be the Chief with some Shells Around his Shoulders we rowed down a little farther down the Gulf and landed upon the Main for to get some Water we found plenty of fresh Water we saw a small Town of Huts about 20 of them just by were the fresh Water was there was none of the Inhabitants in their Huts or about them that we Could see their Huts was large enough for six or seven of them to Stand upright in they were made of Bark and Covered Over with Grass we filled our 2 Breakers with fresh Water and came on board of our Boat again for we were afraid of Staying on Shore for fear of the Natives we went three or four Miles from the Shore and dropt our Killock[2] and there Stopped all Night the next Morng we was detirmened to Go to the same Place to recruit our Water but as we were making to the Shore we saw two very large Canoes coming towards us we did not know what to do for we were afraid to meet them there seemed to us to be 30 or 40 Men in each Canoe they had Sails in their Canoes seemed to made of Matting one of their Canoes was a Head of the others a little Way Stopt untill the other Came up and then she Hoisted her Sails and made after us as soon as we saw that we Tack'd about with what Water we had – Detirmined to Cross the Gulf which was about five Hundred Miles Across which as God wou'd have it we Out run them they followed us until we Lost sight of them we having but little fresh Water and no Wood to make a Fire with but in four days and a half we made the other side of the Gulf we put on Shore to look for some fresh Water but cou'd find none at that Place but we kept along Shore untill the Eveng we saw a small river which we made to and Got Plenty of Fresh Water we put of to Sea the same Night we saw no more Land untill we Came into the Lattitude of North End of the Island we hawled up to make the land to get some fresh Water but saw no Land but a heavy Swell running which had liked to have swallowed us up then

---

[1] Carpentaria.   [2] anchor.

we Concluded as the best Way to shape our Course for the Island of Timor with what little Water we had which we made it in 36 hours after we which we run along the Island of Timor till we came to the Dutch Settlements where we went on Shore to the Governors house where he behaved extremelye well to us filled our Bellies and Cloathed Double with every that was wore on the Island which we remd very happy at our work for two Months till Wm Bryant had words With his wife went and informed against himself Wife and Children and all of us which we was immediately taken Prisoners and was put into the Castle we were strictly Examined after been Examined we were allowed to Go out of the Castle 2 at a time for one Day and the next Day 2 more and so we continued until Captain Edwards who had been on search of the Bounty Pirates which had taken some of the Pirates at Otaheite which he lost the Pandora frigate betwixt New Guinea and New Holland which he made Island of Timor in the Pinnace Two yawls and his Long boat and 120 hands which was saved which Captain Edwards came to us to know what we were which we told him we was Convicts and had made our Escape from Botany Bay which he told us we was his prisoners and put us on board the Rambang Dutch Companys Ship and put us Both Legs in Irons Called the bilboes which we was Conveyed to bretava[1] which we was taken out of the Rambang and put on board a Dutch Guardship in Irons again there we Lost the Child 6 days after the father of the Child was taken Bad and Died which was both buried at Bretava 6 weeks after we was put on 3 different Ships bound to the Cape of Good hope which we was 3 months before we reachd the Cape when we came there the Gorgon man of war which had brought the marines from Botany Bay which we was Put on board of Gorgon which we was known well by all the marine officers which was all Glad that we had not perished at sea was brought home to England in the Gorgon we was Brought ashore at Purfleet and from there Conveyed by the Constables to Bow st office London and was taken before Justice Bond and was fully committed to Newgate ! Wm Moatton Navigatoter of the Boat died James Cox Died Saml Burd Died Wm Bryant Died A Boy of 12 months old Died A little girl 3 Yrs and a Quarter old died the mother of the 2 Children Mary Bryant alive James Martin alive Wm Allen alive John Brown alive Nathl Lilly alive.

[1] Batavia.

Bibliography

MANUSCRIPT DOCUMENTS

IN PUBLIC RECORD OFFICE

Assizes, 24/26: Transportation Order Book, 1771–89. Conviction and sentence of transportation on Mary Broad and on William Bryant.

Assizes, 23/8: Gaol Book for Western Circuit. Mary Broad to be hanged; reprieved and to be transported. William Bryant to be hanged; Reprieved and to be transported.

Assizes, 21/12: Western Circuit Assize.

Adm., 2/120: Captain Edwards' Sailing Orders.

Adm., 51/383: Contains Log of HMS *Gorgon*.

H.O.: 26/1: Newgate Register. 'Transports at large' lodged in Newgate, including 'Mary Briant alias Broad'.

H.O.: 26/56: July Sessions, 1792. Prisoners in Newgate.

Register of Royal Pardons, April and May, 1793, p. 57.

IN MITCHELL LIBRARY, SYDNEY, N.S.W.

Captain W. Bligh's Log of a Voyage in HMS *Providence*, 1793.

Lieutenant G. Tobin's Journal of a Voyage in HMS *Providence*, 1793. (Both this and Captain Bligh's Log refer to the story of the Bryants' escape and arrival at Coupang.)

LIST OF PRINTED BOOKS CONSULTED

ADMIRALTY. *Sailing Directions*. Various volumes.

— *Wind and Current Charts*.

ANTHONY, I. *Saga of the Bounty, its strange history as related by the participants themselves*. London, 1935.

BARROW, SIR J. *The Mutiny and Piratical Seizure of H.M.S. Bounty*. London, 1914.

BECKE, L., and JEFFREY, W. *A First Fleet Family*. London, 1896.

BELCHER, LADY. *Mutineers of the Bounty and their descendants in Pitcairn and Norfolk Islands*. London, 1870.

BLIGH, WILLIAM. *Narrative of the Mutiny on Board His Majesty's Ship Bounty, and subsequent Voyage in the Ship's Boat from Tofoa ... to Timor.... London, 1790.

— *A Voyage to the South Sea*. London, 1792.

BONE, DAVID W. *The Brassbounder*. London, 1949.

BONNOR SMITH, D. 'Some Remarks about the Mutiny of the *Bounty*'. *Mariner's Mirror*, vol. XXII, no. 2, April 1936.

— 'More Light on Bligh and the *Bounty*'. *Mariner's Mirror*, April 1937, pp. 210–28.

CARTERET, ADMIRAL P. 'An Account of a Voyage Round the World.' In J. Hawkesworth, *Account of the Voyages . . . by Byron, Wallis, Carteret, and Cook*, vol. I, London, 1773.

CLOWES, W. L. *The Royal Navy: a history*. 7 vols. London, 1897–1903.

COLLINS, D. *An Account of the English Colony in New South Wales*. 2 vols. London, 1798–1802.

CORNEY, B. G. *The Quest and Occupation of Tahiti*, by emissaries of Spain during the years 1772–6, told in despatches and other contemporary documents; translated and compiled by B. G. Corney. 3 vols. Hakluyt Society, Works, Series II, nos 32, 36, 43, London, 1913–19.

DAMPIER, WILLIAM. *Collection of Voyages*. 4 vols. London, 1729.

EDWARDS, E. *Voyage of H.M.S.* Pandora. Despatched to arrest the mutineers of the *Bounty* in the South Seas, 1790–1, being the narratives of Captain Edwards RN, the Commander, and George Hamilton, the Surgeon. With an introduction and notes by Sir Basil Thomson. London, 1915.

GOULD, LIEUT.-COM. *William Bligh's Notes on Cook's Last Voyage*. *Mariner's Mirror*, vol. XIV, no. 4, October 1928.

HAMILTON, GEORGE A. *Voyage Round the World in H.M. Frigate* Pandora. Performed under the direction of Captain Edwards, 1790–2; with the discoveries made in the South Sea and . . . a Voyage of Eleven Hundred Miles in Open Boats, between Endeavour Straits and the Island of Timor. Berwick, 1793.

LEE, IDA. *Captain Bligh's Second Voyage to the South Seas*. London, 1906 and 1920.

MARTIN, J. *Memorandoms*. Edited by C. Blount. London, 1937.

MCFARLAND, A. *Mutiny in the* Bounty *and Story of the Pitcairn Islanders*. Sydney, 1884.

MACKANESS, G. *Life of Admiral Bligh*. 2 vols. Sydney, 1931.

MONTGOMERIE, H. S. *The Morrison Myth*, a pendant to William Bligh of the *Bounty*, in Fact and in Fable, 1938.

MORRISON, J. *Journal of James Morrison*, Boatswain's Mate of the *Bounty*, describing the Mutiny and Subsequent Misfortunes of the Mutineers; together with an Account of the Island of Tahiti. With an Introduction by Owen Rutter. London, 1935.

MORTIMER, G. *Observations and Remarks made during a voyage to the islands of . . . Otaheite . . . in the brig Mercury*. London, 1791.

NICOLAS, SIR N. H. *Dispatches and Letters of Lord Nelson*. 7 vols. London, 1844–6.

NOTABLE BRITISH TRIALS. *Court Martial of the* Bounty *Mutineers*. London, 1931.

O'HARA, J. *History of New South Wales*. London, 1817.

RAWSON, GEOFFREY. *Bligh of the* Bounty. London, 1930.

RUTTER, OWEN. *True Story of the Mutiny of the* Bounty. London, 1936.

— 'Bligh's Log.' *Mariner's Mirror*, vol. XXII, no. 2, April, 1936.

— *Turbulent Journey: A Life of William Bligh*. London, 1936.

TAGART, E. *A Memoir of the Late Captain Peter Heywood, RN.* London, 1832.

TENCH, CAPTAIN WATKIN. *A Narrative of the Expedition to Botany Bay.* London, 1879.

— *A Complete Account of the Settlement at Port Jackson.* London, 1793.

WALLIS, CAPTAIN S. *The History of Wallis's and Carteret's Voyage Round the World.* London, 1784.

WHITE, JOHN. *Journal of a Voyage to New South Wales.* London, 1790.

WILSON, CAPTAIN J. *First Missionary Voyage to the South-sea Islands, performed in the ship* Duff. Universal Navigator, London, 1805.

Index

Admiralty, the, and Bligh, 3; appoints Edwards to *Pandora*, 4–5, 94
Adventure HMS, 9, 14
Aguila, the, 9, 14, 28n[1]
Aitutaki, 19, 27n[1], 78
Allen, William, 130, 135, 139–40, 149, 154
Anaa (Chain) Island, 8n
Anamooka, 81, 82, 83, 84, 86, 124–5
Assistant, HMS, 92
Astrolabe, the, 90

Barrow, Sir John, his *Eventful History*, 66, 145, 148
Batavia, 129–31, 154
Beechey, Captain F. W., *Narrative . . .*, 76
Bentham, Gregory, 6, 104, 105, 106, 130
Blenheim, HMS, 147
Bligh, Captain, 5, 6, 15, 19, 22, 24, 50–1, 89, 95, 110n[1], 125, 127; reports loss of the *Bounty*, 3; criticisms of, 11, 66, 148; on Tahiti, 28, 30n[2], 34, 41n, 45, 50, 60, 75 and n; and Mortimer, 29; his *Narrative of the Mutiny*, 37–8, 109, 142, 148; and the deserters, 43–4, 57; and Fryer, 46–7; and the responsibility for the mutiny, 48, 54, 57, 58, 102n; and Heywood, 48–9, 102n; and the cause of the mutiny, 68; and Torres Strait, 92, 94; his boat journey compared with Edwards', 108–9; at Coupang, 118 and n[1]; and the Fijis, 126
Boenechea, Captain Domingo de, 8n, 9, 10, 14, 28 and n[1]
Bone, Sir David, *The Brassbounder*, 62–3
Boswell, James, and Mary Bryant, 140–1

Boudeuse, the 8, 68, 73, 77
Bougainville, Louis Antoine de, 8, 14, 68, 73, 76
Bounty, HMS, 15, 22, 92; reported lost by mutiny, 3–4; her mission, 11; Christian assumes command, 18; at Tubuai Island, 18–19, 19–20; at Tahiti, 19, 20–1, 65n; her chronometer, 22, 24; Cox and, 27; chronology of her movements, 34; events of the mutiny, 43–4, 63; deserters from, 43–4; Edwards' search for, 78–88; at Tofoa, 82, 83; court martial of the mutineers, 142–5; accounts of the mutiny, 148
Brown, J., A.B., on Tahiti, 30–3, 44, 71 and n[2]; joins *Pandora*, 50, 59
Bryant, Charlotte, 122, 130, 132, 135, 136, 137, 138–9
Bryant, Emmanuel, 121, 122, 129 and n, 130
Bryant, Mary, 121–2, 129, 130, 132, 135, 136–7; her fate, 138–41, 140n[1], 154
Bryant, William, 120–2, 129 and n, 130, 131, 154
Burkitt, Thomas, 47, 101, 102; and the mutiny, 57; his fate, 142, 143
Butcher, John, 130, 135, 139–40, 149 and n[1]
Byrne, Michael, 20, 40, 47, 101, 102; his arrest, 50–1; his fate, 142–3
Byron, George Gordon, Lord, *The Island*, 5, 41–2, 73–4
Byron, Captain John, 10, 80 and n

Carrington, *Discovery of Tahiti*, 70
Carteret, Captain, 16, 89; and Pitcairn Island, 22, 25
Charlotte, HMS, 121, 137, 138, 149
Cherry, Mr, 105

161

Index

Index

Salote, Queen, 88, 89
Samarang, 122, 123, 127–8
Schouten, Captain Willem, 88–9
Simms, John, 130, 132–3
Sivall, John, 79
Skinner, Richard, 40, 46, 47, 101, 102, 104, 143; his arrest, 47
Smith, Alexander, 24
Spain, 3; and Tahiti, 8–9, 68, 77; loses the Pacific, 10–11
Staines, Captain Sir Thomas, 16, 24
Stewart, George, 18, 20, 40, 46, 101, 102 and n, 104, 143; his wife and child, 40, 41–2, 64; his arrest, 47
Sumner, John, 47, 57, 102, 104, 143

Table Bay, 133, 134
Tagart, E., *Memoir of . . . Heywood*, 49, 101
Tahiti, 4; its discovery and occupation, 8–10; expeditions to, 14–15, 41n, 69; Christian returns to, 19–21; the *Mercury* and, 26–9; its chief, 34–5, 146; rival chiefs of, 52–3; its romantic interest, 68–9, 72, 75–6; blood sacrifices, 71; practical communism, 71–2; its idyllic state, 73–4; impact of Western civilization on, 75–7
Taiarapu, 45n
Tamarie *see* Pomare
Taroa, 20, 21
Tasman, Abel Janszoon, 126
Tench, Captain Watkin, 137 and n[2], 138

Thompson, Matthew, 40, 43; murders Churchill, 44; killed by natives, 45
Thomson, Sir Basil, 26n, 36, 41n; and Captain Edwards, 11–12, 15 and n, 16, 94, 95, 99, 109; and the mutineers, 20n; on the Friendly Islands, 86–7; and Mary Bryant, 140 and n[1]
Tikopia Island, 90
Timor, 39, 106, 109, 117, 154
Tinah, Chief, *see* Otoo
Tinkler, Robert, A.B., 47n
Tofoa Island, 28n[2], 82–4, 88, 124–5
Tonga *see* Friendly Islands
Toobou, Chief, 82, 83, 88
Torres Strait, 91, 92–5, 109
Tubuai Island, 18–20, 27, 78

Uea Island, 89
Union Group, 80 and n
Upolu, 81, 83, 84, 123–4

Vanikoro Island, 90
Vanion, Mynheer, 118 and n, 127
Venereal disease, in Tahiti, 75, 76–7

Wallis, Captain, 89; and Tahiti, 8, 9, 14, 68, 69, 76
Warrior, HMS, 29
Wilson, J., *Missionary Voyage*, 64
Women, of Tahiti, 68–9, 70–2, 74; of Anamooka, 86